HV851.C64

COLLINS
FAMILY DAY CARE

DATE DUE

WITHDRAWN FROM THE EVANS
LIBRARY AT FMCC

DATE DUE			
f/10/77			
DEC 16 '91			
DEC 16 '91			
MAR 10 '93			
APR 10 '95			
NOV 2 2006			

FULTON-MONTGOMERY COMMUNITY
COLLEGE LIBRARY

FAMILY DAY CARE

FAMILY DAY CARE

A PRACTICAL GUIDE FOR

PARENTS,

CAREGIVERS, AND PROFESSIONALS

ALICE H. COLLINS / EUNICE L. WATSON

BEACON PRESS   BOSTON

Copyright © 1976 by Alice Collins and Eunice Watson

Beacon Press books are published under the auspices of the Unitarian Universalist Association

Published simultaneously in Canada by Fitzhenry & Whiteside Limited, Toronto

All rights reserved

Printed in the United States of America

(hardcover) 9 8 7 6 5 4 3 2 1

For permission to reprint in this book, the authors are grateful to the following: Mav Pardee for an excerpt from *Playgroups: How to Grow Your Own,* Child Resource Center, Cambridge, Mass.; June Sale for an excerpt from "A Self-Help Organization of Family Day Care Mothers as a Means of Quality Control"; and Anita Yoskowitz for an excerpt from *Playgroups—Do It Ourselves Childcare,* Childcare Switchboard/Single Parent Reserve Center, San Francisco.

Library of Congress Cataloging in Publication Data

Collins, Alice H.
   Family day care.
   Includes bibliographical references and index.
   1. Day care centers—Handbooks, manuals, etc.
I. Watson, Eunice L., joint author. II. Title.
HV851.C64   362.7'1   75-36039
ISBN 0-8070-3158-5

*To Susan Berresford, whose imagination and interest
made it possible for us to meet some
of the many generous and talented people
who contributed to this book*

CONTENTS

Introduction   ix

1 Informal Family Day Care for Working Parents   1

What family day care is. Givers and users speak for themselves. Finding family day care givers. Recognizing the needs of givers.

2 Co-op Child Care Exchanges and Playgroups   23

Organizing co-op child care exchanges. Organizing Playgroups. Communal child care.

3 Public Family Day Care   34

A Welfare mother as day care giver. The evolution of public family day care. Public family day care: dream and reality.

4 Information and Referral Services   46

Building a bridge for users and givers. Informal information and referral. Developing a comprehensive service. Satellite information and referral services.

5 Associations: Family Day Care Givers Organize   58

How Associations developed. What Associations can do. A profile of WATCH (Women Attentive to Children's Happiness).

6 The Day Care Neighbor Service   72

What the Day Care Neighbor Service is. Planning a Day Care Neighbor Service. Helping Day Care Neighbors take an official role. Building a firm partnership. Helping Day Care Neighbors with maintenance problems. Using additional communications avenues.

7 Licensing   113

The stormy emergence of licensing. Problems and pitfalls of licensing. Positive results.

8 Training   124

Teaching the talented. Training programs that work.

Envoi   137

Index   139

INTRODUCTION

This book is a result of our experience in developing an innovative family day care programs and our recent national survey of family day care sponsored by the Ford Foundation. It is an effort to put together some of what we have learned from many sources in such a way that it will be useful to the families of young children—those who want to have their children cared for in the homes of other families, whether for full- or part-time, from choice or necessity. And it should also be helpful to their opposite numbers who want to add to family income and feel themselves a part of the life around them while remaining in their own homes caring for the children of others.

We would like it to be useful too to professionals who plan and administer programs of family day care. And it would be satisfying if it could help shape policy in health and safety, education and community planning—all touched, in a greater or lesser way, by family day care—that growing American social custom.

To keep the book within manageable limits, we have avoided citing well-known statistics of present and projected need and arguments perpetuating historic debates about the relative virtues of one kind of care over another. We have assumed that to meet the wonderful variety of lifestyles in this country there must be a wide choice of child care arrangements, and that, for the most part, the families directly concerned are the best judges of the "fit" between what exists and what their needs are, and that the joint activities of all concerned, professionals and laypeople, can develop the services presently missing.

The choice of subjects and their distillation has not been easy, since we have been so constantly aware that such choices are not only arbitrary but may reflect our own prejudices and enthusiasms.

We regret most of all that we cannot give due credit to the many people who shaped the ideas in this book and are going on working to develop these and many others which will be of interest. Most interviewees found it easier to talk freely if they could be assured anonymity. And others feared that if they were named, they would receive requests for materials no longer in print, perhaps even addressed to agencies and services no longer in existence. Having had some firsthand unhappy experiences in this regard, we agreed to "name no names" except with express permission. We do pledge, however, that when expressing a personal, and not a composite opinion, we will make this clear in the text. We regret even more that our promise to preserve anonymity forbids listing the many people who have contributed to these pages by sharing their time and knowledge with the writers—and the readers. It does not, however, inhibit our unreserved gratitude and appreciation.

FAMILY DAY CARE

CHAPTER 1

INFORMAL FAMILY DAY CARE FOR WORKING PARENTS

What Family Day Care Is

In this chapter we will show what informal family day care is chiefly by letting givers and users speak for themselves.

The comments of family day care givers and users quoted in these pages are taken from taped interviews carried on in two consecutive projects that sought to discover what family day care is really like—though the official titles of the studies were somewhat more formidable.*

The studies were a response to demands for more and better day care of all kinds, raised by many voices, and setting widely divergent standards. Health, education and welfare agencies saw good day care as a means of preventive intervention with very young children who would otherwise be handicapped for life, emotionally and physically. Employers of women in industry, business and the professions saw it as essential to securing a dependable work force. Taxpayers, through their representatives, saw it as a means of decreasing the dependency of families with young children. Mothers who worked from choice or necessity knew that their working lives had to be built on a base of good child care. And other mothers, perhaps for a wider range of reasons and under less pressure, were anxious to find children to care for while they remained at home with their own.

Since most of these groups had little contact with each other, each

The Day Care Exchange Project, Children's Bureau Child Welfare and Demonstration Grants Program, OWR6. D-135 and *Field Study of the Neighborhood Family Day Care System*, Children's Bureau Research Grant, R-287, Office of Child Development, HEW.

saw a different part of the whole and, like the famous story of the blind men and the elephant, each thought the part they touched suggested a beast very different from that described by their neighbors.

For example, census figures disclosed that almost half the working force were mothers which made it likely that what they wanted for their children was some form of day care. But studies of existing facilities showed they were often under-enrolled though aware of demand far beyond their capacity. With the allocation of large sums of tax money to day nursery programs, the percentage of children of working mothers cared for in this way changed only a few percentage points from the original ten percent the first studies had revealed. Nor did it help to look at officially sanctioned family day care—so small a proportion of children were cared for by such facilities, even in states where penalties for noncompliance were high, that they were "not statistically significant."

So perhaps the remaining children were cared for as they had traditionally been, at home, by servants or relatives? The former hardly need be discussed, let alone investigated. A quick check revealed that those traditional babysitters, the grandmothers, were themselves likely to be in the labor force.

Certainly with the wide diversity in vocational hours, some children could be cared for by their parents, with mothers and fathers adjusting working schedules so that one was at home with the children at all times. But what about the divorce rate, the very high incidence of single parents—where were their children and how were they being cared for? The special census reports indicated that they, like many of those with intact families, were being cared for in family homes of non-relatives, through arrangements made between the two families.

And this raised a whole new set of questions. What kind of care was being found and used outside of agency auspices? Should it be sanctioned—and if so, how far, and with what kind of funds, under what kinds of conditions? What was it *really* like—and did it work? How did people wanting to use family day care find those wanting to give it? What happened when they found each other? Those and a host of other questions clamored for answers if future planning was to make good provision for this ever growing, vital and vulnerable population—young children with working parents.

Our first study, the Day Care Exchange Project, was funded as a demonstration and research project of a new kind of child welfare service. The site was in a neighborhood with a wide social and economic range within relatively narrow geographic boundaries. Informal observations which preceded the project left no doubt that working mothers at every level there wanted reliable care for their young children in nearby homes. It seemed obvious that they would be delighted to use a service that would help them find this care. But what did day care givers want that would motivate them to undertake to meet the requirements of membership in the projected exchange? Curiously enough, no studies of day care *givers*—even of just what day care giving was—existed as guides.

So the Day Care Exchange (soon to be renamed the Day Care Neighbor Service) decided to begin learning some of what went into giving care by asking day care givers in the project neighborhood about it. Dire predictions of the difficulties of getting givers to talk freely to strangers were not borne out, perhaps because of genuine interest in young children and families and their pleasure to find someone interested in hearing their viewpoint. Those interviews led to a change from the original plan to the Day Care Neighbor Service described in Chapter Six and to the greatly enlarged and carefully controlled field study. When all the data were in, and the pieces put together, we hoped to have a picture of what informal family day care (that carried on without recourse to professional service) *is*—not what it *should* be, or *might* be, but what it *is* right now, today.

How the information was collected does need a further word of explanation. Successful studies of social behavior seem to be made when researchers enter the new country as unobtrusively as possible, show their genuine interest and good will, and ask questions when the time seems right. For purposes of research, it is necessary to have answers to questions which can be compared to each other and also to have spontaneous responses and insights—the threads that weave the cloth of all human interaction. Information about family day care in the projects was collected not only by these means but through "participant observers," the individuals especially knowledgeable about their communities and especially interested in young families—the Day Care Neighbors (*see* Chapter 6).

To illustrate what informal family day care is, and perhaps to certify the term, we have chosen in the following pages a few nuggets from the gold mine of thousands of taped, transcribed materials taken from the natural culture of family day care. The interviews have been condensed and edited, and of course disguised, omitting much of the chitchat about the weather and other small talk and some of the wording of casual speech—but not without pain to the writers to whom these sometimes long-winded passages, gave invaluable insights into the living reality of this flourishing form of social interaction.

Givers and Users Speak for Themselves

1

Mother: We used to live here when I was a kid and then last spring when Mike was out of work, we decided to come back here because there were supposed to be jobs, but he couldn't find anything. So we decided I better go back to work—I haven't worked since we were married, but I'm a telephone operator and I knew I could get a job—but first we had to find a babysitter for Shelley. We didn't like the idea—she's two—but then...

So I asked my grandmother—she still lives here and she isn't too old or anything like that—but she had a job at the plant so that was out. Then I went over to the high school—I've only been out three years and I know a lot of the kids still, see, but no luck. And then one of them told her friend about me. They live just a few blocks down so Mike went to talk to her and she said she would take Shelley, so we felt a lot better.

But then the only job hours I could get was four P.M. to midnight, which was fine while Mike was out of a job, but he got one from seven A.M. to three-thirty P.M. pretty quick. Velma—that's our babysitter—she wouldn't keep Shelley after four-thirty because that's when her husband comes home and he doesn't like to have kids around then—maybe they like to drink beer or just make out for a while—they don't have kids. She's a real nice girl but she wouldn't change those hours one bit.

So my mother was at me to quit work but I really liked working again and they promised me the next day shift that comes up—those shifts do change a lot because the girls take leaves and quit and stuff. My mother doesn't understand it—she was always staying home with us—but I really like getting out, seeing the girls, having a little extra money to spend, though we're going to try and save most of mine. Still it *is* mine and if I want something dumb like a pair of crazy shoes or something...

Of course I wouldn't do it if Shelley wasn't getting good care but, honest, Velma is better with babies than I am. She says she's taking care of Shelley because she wants one of her own so bad and her husband says they're too much trouble—she says she's trying to sort of break him in to the idea of a baby and he is getting so he plays with Shelley and even takes her for a walk sometimes if he gets off early.

It's funny, she's having better luck potty-training her than I have. She says she had a lot of little sisters and so she knows about kids. I was an only child and my mother was divorced so I wasn't around babies but, boy, I knew I wanted one of my own and to bring it up different. So this works out fine for us—like Shelley has sort of relations. Mike picks her up now, but I'm getting changed to days next month. I kind of hope Velma doesn't get pregnant too soon.

2

Mother works in an electronic manufacturing plant. Girl, 5, boy, 8.

Mother: The children both go to the babysitter around seven when I go to work and stay till eight-thirty and then my little girl goes to kindergarten and Joey goes to school in the same building so he walks her. The sitter picks her up at eleven-thirty and then Joey goes there after school till I get them on my way home from work.

Usually they go five days a week but lately my husband's been out of work so he's been sitting with them. She'll be glad when he gets back to work so she'll get the money again—and so will I!

Interviewer: Did you know her before she began sitting for you?

Mother: Well, I wouldn't say I knew her exactly—I met her at my sister's a couple of years ago—just to talk to. That's at the other end of the school district. I knew some people closer to the kids' school and I would have liked that, but we don't have a car and I was in the hospital last year with back trouble so I couldn't walk them that far and we didn't know where he would be working. Then I met her at the market one day and, as luck would have it, she has a little boy in the same kindergarten class as my daughter. Her husband needs the car so she walks her little boy.

Interviewer: Have you had babysitting arrangements before?

Mother: Oh yeah—good and bad ones. One the boy was always crying when I went to get him but there didn't seem anything wrong. He was always clean and wasn't hungry or anything and she seemed like a nice woman and she didn't complain about him. I still don't know what it was. But my boyfriend—I wasn't married then—said a kid oughtn't to act like that and to find another sitter and I did and it went a lot better.

And then there was one place—I liked it real good—the sitter lived with her mother and if the sitter wanted to go out, the mother would take care of the kids. With the two of them I could just forget all about worrying about waking up in the morning and finding the babysitter was sick and then what do you do? But they'd rather take kids not school age because they need the money—they can take up to six on their license, and that adds up and for mine now I don't pay such a lot, so . . . But it isn't much trouble for the lady I have now either because she has to do it with her own children anyway and her husband has a good job so I think this one will last.

3

Giver: This is the third week I've been taking care of Susan—she's almost one and I have her the full day two days a week from seven-thirty to five-fifteen and the rest from eight to five-thirty. See, my little girl is nine months so I'm up anyway. It's funny, I have a couple of other kids I take care of once in a while when their mothers have to leave for an appointment or something and those little girls—they don't like it! They can't even walk good, but they roll in front of any strange kid and keep it away from a toy. There's a little Japanese boy, he's about three—he's just adorable. He comes about once a week or two weeks. His mother goes shopping and leaves him because he likes to come. And sometimes she just comes by and says, "Can I leave him? He doesn't want to stay with me!" He's too big for the little girls to pester so they all just play where they want with a little fight over a toy once in a while.

Interviewer: How long had you known your regular one... Jan?... her mother before you decided to babysit for her?

Giver: I didn't know her at all, but the day they came over, I found out he is working where I was working when I got pregnant. So I know all the people he works with and where he works and all. She's in training and is going into the same office. We had a lot in common, but I hadn't known them at all. However, now we've—our husbands see each other because John brings the little girl quite often. And one night when they both came to get her, we ended up all of us, including the babies, going out for pizza. They're real nice.

Interviewer: How did they find you?

Giver: Through the day care center, I guess. See, about November I got to thinking about buying my husband a Christmas present so I put an ad in the paper to babysit because I didn't think I wanted to leave my little girl and go back to work. The center only takes older kids there, but they took my name because they said they often had calls looking for care—especially babies and I guess that's how they found me. I had some other calls, too.

Interviewer: Why did you choose this one?

Giver: I liked the parents because they were particular. See, they both wanted to come over and meet me and they asked if they could discuss some things and if they did leave her, could they come sometimes and visit. They let the little girl wander around and get acquainted. It was very nice. This type of people, you know they take their girl to the doctor regularly and she gets a bath every day and you know they'll pick her up after work. You just know, that's all.

And then they said they would like to bring her once more before they left her all day so she wouldn't be frightened and I thought that was great. Actually, they came two more times and just stayed a little while. I was very impressed with their attitude because this was my feeling—how could I leave my little girl with a total stranger—I'd want to go over there just like they did.

And they had lists of all the things I would have asked for—doctors to call and places I could reach them and all.

Interviewer: You said you had other calls you didn't take—why was that?

Giver: Well, one woman called, divorced, working at the Food Mart, had a couple of children she wanted me to care for. And if she happened to have a date, could she leave them longer? "If she happened to have a date!" She didn't sound at all like something I'd be interested in, so I told her, "Your children are really too old for my daughter and my husband goes to work at five A.M. and so we go to bed early and that wouldn't work with your working evenings at the Food Mart."

Interviewer: How long do you think you'll go on with the arrangement you have now?

Giver: I don't know. At first, I was only going to do it on a temporary basis, because I didn't want to be tied down after I earned the money I wanted. But I'm really not. The girls get along so well, I just take them both, the way I'd do mine before I had the two. I think I'll do it till her parents want to change, or whatever—I'll wait and see.

Interviewer: Did you talk about this when you took her?

Giver: Yes. They didn't want somebody who was just going to take her for two or three weeks. They were worried about leaving her with a different sitter every week. And I said I wouldn't make any promises because the little girls might be unhappy with each other and then I wouldn't keep her or if she cried all day or something. We had a rough week the first one, but I felt you couldn't judge by that and the second week she was so happy to come on Monday she got so excited, her mother said. Honestly, they'd missed each other. But the first week was hard. She's just at the age when she likes to have her mother around.

And then, my husband has a schedule that once in a while he gets a couple of days off in the middle of the week and we like to go off some place in our camper so I told them that, and they said they would always be willing to make arrangements to leave her with an aunt or something if it was just for a few days. So I don't feel I have to have her every day, every week, every month, and that makes it nice. Like one night my daughter began running a high temperature and I called them early in the morning and said it was up to them. I'd take her, but if it was the other way around, I wouldn't want them to bring her here. So she didn't come for two days and I was glad, because I really wanted to spend all my time with my little girl—she was real sick. Still, I wouldn't have wanted to leave them stranded or maybe lose her job for her either.

Interviewer: Do you ever get chatting about other things like your own families?

Giver: Oh, yes, it's really strange how much we have in common—like both of our husbands have been married before and both of them have a child by the previous marriage and neither of us really like that much. As a matter of fact, we just laugh all the time about how much we have in common in this way.

And we've worked out the money. At first she was going to bring her little girl's food and take home the diapers to do, but babies don't eat much and I have to do my own diapers every day anyway so she just pays me fifty cents a week more than we'd agreed on and brings the milk, and it works out with less trouble for us both.

Interviewer: How does your husband feel about your babysitting?

Giver: Well, when we were first married, we decided he'd go to school and I'd work and that's what we did, but I got pregnant pretty soon. Tell you the truth, I think I was kind of careless about the pill because I really like being home more than working and I always wanted children. My husband didn't mind—he makes enough money for us to live okay. Of course it isn't fancy, but he takes care of it and I spend anything I make, any way I want. His first wife worked—she went to work four weeks after the baby was born—and their marriage lasted about six months. We don't have everything in the world, but our marriage is going great. I could work part-time for my father and someday I will, but for now, this suits us all great.

4

Mother: I've had to quit work. I'm a legal secretary and I've never missed work or anything, even with the three children, except just for short maternity leaves—but I'm going to have to stay home now with my middle boy. He was in a real bad accident on his bike. He's going to have to be in bed for six months at least and after that it will be a long time till he's all right so I don't have any choice. I hated to tell my babysitter. She's taken care of all my kids for years and he's almost like hers, too, and she feels so badly. She used to go see him in the hospital while I was still working and before I knew I was going to have to quit.

Interviewer: I'm certainly sorry to hear that he is having such a bad time—it's so hard for active kids. But maybe you'll at least have a lot less pressure on you, keeping up the kind of house you do and working too—I've wondered how you ever manage.

Mother: Well, to tell you the truth, I think I'll find it harder to stay home than go to work! That's why I started in the first place. You know, my husband's a lawyer and we don't need the money I make, though it's nice to have the kids' education all salted away. But I just got so restless at home—I love the kids, that's why we have them— but being with them all day just drove me nuts. And I used to work and I'm good at it and I like it. I used to think I was awful to feel that way, but then I went to a class reunion—our fifth—and half my classmates seemed to feel the same way—it was really funny.

Interviewer: Were most of them working?

Mother: I thought so, but maybe I just wanted to think so. Anyway, I talked it over with my husband and he was sort of upset, I guess, like I wanted to leave him and them. But we got that straightened out and he said I could if I could find someone we'd both approve of. It took awhile—we answered ads, and we asked a lot of friends and we even called one of those agencies that are like employment agencies and finally a friend told us about a friend of hers who was awfully good with kids and wasn't crazy about going to work, but was thinking about it because her oldest kid was in school and she is an R.N. and was getting a lot of calls from hospitals to come back to work. Anyway, that was three years ago and they've been there ever since.

Interviewer: I guess you've gotten to be good friends in that long time?

Mother: Well, no, I really wouldn't say that. She has her friends and we have ours. We like each other, but we don't see each other except when my husband or I ferry the kids back and forth. If there is something about them, we sure talk about it, but not about ourselves. There really isn't any reason to.

Interviewer: Will the others stay home with you now, too?

Mother: I've been thinking about it a lot and I want to talk to her about it. I'm sort of scared of going back full-time to being tied to the house but of course I will be anyway with poor Pete and maybe having the other kids would break up the monotony for him—or maybe it would upset him that they can do what they want and he can't. I don't know. For now, we've agreed they'll stay with her till I get us organized here and then we'll see . . . maybe just part-time or maybe she'll take them once in a while. They'll miss her, too . . .

5

Giver: I've got a new baby to take care of—she's just a doll. Jan works and Don is at the community college and it runs a little day nursery and they thought they could leave her there, but they only take kids over three. I know a woman who works and she told them to call me. It isn't regular—I wouldn't have taken another full-time, one is enough with my own three—but it's only some hours when he's at school. Otherwise, he keeps her.

Interviewer: How does Patti like it?

Giver: Not much at first, but she's getting used to it. She used to go to "love" the baby and be awful rough. I told the Smiths when I first took the baby, "I have a little one you know, and I wouldn't certainly deliberately let her hurt the baby but I can't exactly stand and watch her all the time either." And that was fine with the Smith kids—which is what they are, eighteen, both of them. You can always tell when he brings her and he's been studying and taking care of her—her diapers are on like you'd never believe, her hat's on crooked, and he's all nervous. When they brought her, they didn't want to talk or ask me anything or anything—they just thought, "A baby's a baby," and anyone who has had one can take care of one! I kid them about it now.

(Two months later.)

Yeah, I have the Smiths still—I sort of think of them all as the baby! Those kids are really so irresponsible. Every once in a while they forget to let me know they aren't bringing her at the regular time—he has vacation or exam weeks or something—so I stay home all day and wait. But they really want to do what's right and I can sort of help them with her. Like last week I said, "It's time you got that kid some new shoes—she's trying to walk and those are a lot too small and they hurt her." "Gee," they said, "thanks. We thought they looked awfully cute, we found them at the flea market, but if they hurt her, she certainly can't wear them."

And they sure forget to pay! I bawled them out last week. It isn't so much that I need the money—but of course that's part of it—but they have to grow up if they've got a kid. They admitted they spent the babysitting money on putting on a big party with their friends. So I gave them a lecture on how bad it is for them and her if they are smoking pot, and they looked real scared and said they weren't that night—though they used to. They really are good kids and they really love that baby—she's the cutest, smartest little thing—so I don't mind kind of acting like a grandmother though I'm a little young for that, my husband likes to say.

6

Giver: I've been taking care of Regina McDaniel's little girl the last four weeks. She's nineteen months and she comes seven-thirty to five-thirty, except on Fridays and I take care of her until seven because of the banks—they don't close until six—so I feed her on Friday, but other than that they pick her up at five-thirty usually.

Interviewer: How many other day care children do you take care of regularly?

Giver: I take care of my niece, who's about two. She usually is here every day but Friday. Her grandmother takes care of her on Friday.

Interviewer: How long have you been caring for her?

Giver: Let's see, it's been a year—I'll say a year because it isn't quite . . .

Interviewer: Do you ever babysit other children?

Giver: No, I haven't yet. A woman called me the other day and said she had a two-year-old boy she'd like me to watch, but I thought I had enough, as it was, right now.

Interviewer: You don't occasionally take care of a neighbor's child in the evening, or . . .

Giver: No, I don't take care of anybody's children in the evening usually.

Interviewer: How many children of your own do you have living at home? Can we start with the youngest?

Giver: There's Alex, two, and Peggy, six, and Tommy is nine, and Judy is ten.

Interviewer: And they're here all the time the day care child is here, or else in school?

Giver: Well, the only one that's actually home is the baby. The other three are here from three o'clock on.

Interviewer: How did you and Regina McDaniel find each other?

Giver: Well, there was an elderly woman who lives down by my mother's restaurant and I was in there with her and my niece, and I had mentioned something about I'd like to keep another child because Christmas money around here with four kids isn't very good. And this Mrs. Howell said, "I know of a girl who needs a babysitter desperately." And she said, "I'll have her call you." Well, she didn't call right away. I think it was almost a month before I heard from her and she called up on a Thursday and then that Friday about ten she came by to see me. We talked for a good two or three hours. We just yakked and yakked and after we got to know each other, it was like we'd known each other for a long time. And the kids played real good, and she decided that as long as her baby would feel at home in the house . . . she asked questions about if I liked children and things like that. And I said, "Naturally," and she just brought her over Monday and I started in.

Interviewer: Did you talk to anyone about deciding to do this?

Giver: Well, my husband. He wanted to know if I thought I could have patience with one that I had never known before, if she could get along with the two I already had, and he wondered if it would shatter my nerves. And I figured it didn't shatter my nerves with my own four, so I think I can pretty well put up with almost anything.

Interviewer: How long do you plan to continue this arrangement?

Giver: Golly, I really couldn't say. She wanted me for what she had said was just a few months to get back on their feet and, I mean, if she wants it to continue, I don't plan on doing it after June, because when my kids come home for summer vacation I want to be with them all the time. And we wouldn't really be able to take them any place and show them anything. If I had to, of course, but I don't think Regina McDaniel would like the idea because I don't keep hers—she'll probably get a high school girl and she'll have vacation some of the time. We usually do quite a bit during the summer vacation. In June I'll just ask her if she will please find somebody else.

Interviewer: Did this subject come up when you were making the arrangement, when she said she would work a few months?

Giver: I didn't say anything to her about it because all she said was that she would be working for a few months only, and I figured well, that was fine, because she doesn't like the idea of working. She'd rather be home with the baby.

Interviewer: Now I'd like to ask you about some of the practical details, things that you felt had to be decided before you began this arrangement. For example, what was the amount of pay decided on?

Giver: Well, I told her that I couldn't do it for less than fifteen dollars a week and she agreed on it—that was fine.

Interviewer: You initiated this?

Giver: Yeah, because I had talked to other women who do it and they say that it's not worth less than three-fifty a day so I thought, well, I'd ask for fifteen dollars. All she could do was say no, she couldn't pay it. But she agreed on it.

Interviewer: If you talked for two or three hours, you must have discussed quite a bit more—

Giver: She asked me if I wouldn't try and toilet-train the baby and I said I might as well because I was trying to do it with my two-year-old. I wasn't having much luck, but I said yes. And then I told her—well, she told me that Kay hadn't been around any other children—and I said about discipline, "I don't like to spank a child, but I can't let yours get away with things that mine can't." And she said fine. She said, "If you think she needs to be punished, you go right ahead." Usually I just make her sit down, and that's punishment enough for her, and usually I don't do it—but she doesn't like the idea of sharing things and I, well, I make mine share, so I have to see if I can't get the idea into her head.

Interviewer: Did you talk about who supplies the food?
Giver: Yes. I told her I would feed the baby lunch and then she said on Fridays, when I feed her dinner, that she would give me an extra dollar.
Interviewer: Did you discuss the child's likes and dislikes?
Giver: Well, she more or less told me that Kay likes to have everything her way. She said she doesn't like—actually she doesn't know how to get along with—other children. And she said that she is liable to try and get away with a lot of things that she couldn't do at home. So, I would have to more or less judge for myself when she was stretching things a little bit too far.
Interviewer: As of now, in what ways is this arrangement what you are looking for?
Giver: Well, it's fine as far as that goes, because I'm not really doing anything more than what I do with mine. I stay home anyway, so it's not a burden on me. And I mean, like I said, I love children and just having her around, it does a lot of good for mine and it does a lot of good for my little niece because she's the only child in her family, too. And they're just like they were always together, you know, all the time, night and day. I think it's wonderful, myself—I mean, I'm helping her, she's helping me, and I think she's very sweet. Regina is just a real mother, she is just, like we say, she's an idiot like I am. And I have met her husband—let's see, he brought the baby over the first time—and he's not very talkative, but then men really aren't.
Interviewer: In what ways was it different from what you were hoping for?
Giver: Well, it really isn't any different. I thought when I first saw the baby, "Golly, maybe she's going to be a problem, and what'll I do and . . ." But she's really no problem at all. I mean, she really is quiet and everything and I couldn't ask for a more perfect arrangement, really. It's worked out pretty good.

Finding Family Day Care Givers

Because arrangements like these are made privately between the two families involved, statistics probably don't begin to measure the number of them. But there are enough figures to suggest that most American children today have had the experience of being taken care of in the home of a nonrelative, or sharing their own home with an unrelated child. This seems to be a relatively new social custom, only reaching noticeable proportions since the Second World War; in reality it is a development of an old social custom.

Young children have always been cared for in the homes of others while their mothers were having babies, nursing a sick member of the family, lending a hand at peak times on the farm, or occupied with other home-based work. Aunts, grandmothers, cousins, even close neighbors, had loose systems of reciprocal child care whereby whoever needed it used it, each giver knowing that when she needed it, it would be offered to her in turn. Usually, the child was just fitted into the caretaking family as another temporary member; sometimes a "special" aunt or cousin provided special activities, outings, and treats. But even in the extended family, today often discussed as a kind of lost paradise, there were instances when children received no better care away from home than they did in their own, marginal families—and sometimes worse.

Family day care, as practised today, developed in a mobile urban society as an extension of earlier forms of care, but for the children of full-time working mothers it is different in significant ways from that of an earlier time. There are considerations of selection, duration, quality of care and purpose, payment, and regulation, which are new.

Most parents would list their greatest problem as "finding a good babysitter."* In the extended family, that was not a problem. It was not always possible to make an arrangement with a relative that was

*This is, perhaps, as good a place as any to deal with the word "babysitter"—which to a semanticist might be a fascinating subject but is a thorn to anyone interested in day care. As a term it is defined in the 1971 Webster's Unabridged Dictionary as "a person engaged usually for pay . . . to take care of a child or children while parents are away from home." A search of the literature on language including slang shows no other definition. One English dictionary explains that this term was originally applied to teenagers but now is in general use. Certainly, it is not its definition that has given the term what most people would agree is a poor reputation even while almost everyone, including babysitters, makes use of it. From the beginning of the project we struggled to find a word to describe the central characters in their work which would make it clear that they had a special role and performed a particular task which was somewhere between a profession, an occupation, and a craft. Labeling their opposite numbers was a bit easier, but men as well as women make use of day

just perfect for all concerned, but at least the parents knew in advance what the advantages and disadvantages were likely to be. Nowadays, the working mother often has to find a stranger and make a decision she does not really feel sure she knows how to make. If she is lucky, she may make the arrangement with a friend, but that arrangement—resembling those in the extended family—is likely to last a rather short time since it is often a friendly gesture of accommodation rather than part of a long range plan. Indeed, one of the reasons why finding a giver is the primary problem of working parents is that, in spite of popular concepts, family day care giving is not thought of as an occupation by most of the women who do it, as the excerpts quoted earlier suggest. They do it when it fits into their own lifestyle and needs—perhaps when their own children are small or have just begun school, leaving a kind of uneasy silence behind them, or when unexpected expenses require additional family income. As these conditions change, most givers terminate their activities and may even become day care users for their school-age children. In the informal, private family day care system, such role switches occur constantly, sensitizing both partners in child care to its problems. The difficulty, however, of finding a day care giver and making a lasting arrangement is a familiar and often uncomfortable factor in the lives of modern families.

The director of an Information and Referral service that handles questions about day care expresses her point of view:

The family day care mother has historically been someone whose own children have grown up and left. Now, I find many people who want to do it are mothers who look at their situation and say, "I'm home anyway with my eighteen-month- or two-year-old child and I want to stay home with this child, but while I'm home I would like to care for other children." So you have a congeniality of mind between the providing mother and the using mother because they are about the same age and they will often turn out to be matched in education. There is not as big a conflict in ideas about child-rearing as there is sometimes if the caregiver is older than the mother or there is a difference in the socio-economic factor.

care facilities. It was decided that family day care user and family day care giver were to be the terms used, and that abbreviation to user and giver would be permissible. Babysitter was ruled out, since it was apparently seen by many as denoting an inferior person performing a menial task. Nevertheless, it often crept back in spoken exchanges, and may lurk in these pages still, in spite of a careful effort to avoid it. There has, of course, been no attempt to change the terms used by others whom we quote.

Most parents would qualify their statement of the problem by saying that it is hard to find a situation where their child or children will be safe and happy, and is feasible for them in terms of payment and accessibility. A few parents will make use of a babysitter who is ideal from the child care point of view but lives an hour's travel away, but there are very few of them. Most parents know that their own happiness has to be considered too if the arrangement is going to be satisfactory and that a long ride morning and evening with a sleepy and/or hungry small child is not going to make anyone's day go more smoothly. The Field Study of the Neighborhood Family Day Care System and other studies have shown that parents prefer a day care arrangement to be within a mile of their home and experience has also strongly suggested that most parents prefer to find the arrangement closer to home than to the job.

A big-city report of day care preferences states:

The career mothers in family day care—and parents interviewed in all major child care demand surveys—make clear the high priority they place on having their children close to home. Parents continually note both the convenience of not having to transport children and infants and the "psychic benefit" of having children close to home. Family day care mothers with children placed in the same apartment building are particularly cognizant of not having to dress toddlers against the cold or take them on subways and buses. Others have spoken of being glad to have their children "in the same community," "near home when older children return from school," "near friends."

"Safe and happy" are terms that mean different things to different families at different times. The parents of a first-grade child might consider a giver's home unsafe while those of a third-grade child will be less concerned that the older children there may be rough playmates, or that there is a stairway unprotected by a gate. And parents who have strong convictions about the importance of nonsexist playthings or natural foods might feel that their child would be happy in a home where their ideas are shared. A family which includes the children in responsibility, or feels the development of intellectual powers is the key to happiness, will seek a different kind of giver than the family that believes little children are happiest when they are free to discover the world for themselves in a permissive, "mothering" environment.

Recognizing the Needs of Givers

The other necessary partner in a family day care arrangement, the caregiver, is likely to feel that the greatest problem is finding the kind of child she wants to care for, and will probably add that she seeks a child who will fit into her family and whose parents are reliable in terms of hours and payment. Few family day care givers expect to earn their living from giving care, which is realistic since it is a most precarious means of livelihood and only feasible if the sitter takes more children than regulations generally permit and devotes herself almost exclusively to them, without regard to her own family. Most givers take on a child or two to care for and expect that this will not seriously interfere with their usual home-centered activities while providing "extra" income—what women in an earlier period called "pin money"—taking the place of the reciprocal relationship which used to be part of the incentive for giving care in the extended family.

While theoretically the giver does not have as much concern for the well-being of a child of strangers that members of the family had for all the related children, it is true that today's caregivers want to look after children who are well cared for by their parents; studies have shown that a leading reason for the giver's terminating an arrangement is parental neglect of the child. (Close behind is failure of parents to pay on time or stick to agreed hours.)

Family day care givers, then, are in fact hard to find, not because there are few of them—although this may be an increasing reality—but because they are looking for certain characteristics in children they will care for, and they are usually under less pressure to make an arrangement than are parent-users, whose jobs may depend on it.

Another reason why users and givers view finding each other as a major problem is that they do not have or do not know of any means of finding each other in most communities, or of getting an expert's opinion about each other and all day care resources. This subject will be discussed at greater length in Chapter Four. Even after users and givers do find each other, work out the payment, and settle down to an arrangement, things do not necessarily go smoothly. Of course, extended family arrangements weren't as idyllic as nostalgia paints them. There are inevitable frictions between two women who take care of the same young child, and the friction does not simply involve real differences of routine or standards, but is mixed up as well with feelings.

"Sure," said a mother in a group discussion about warmth in babysitters, "I want her to love my kid—but not too much! *I'm* his mother and I don't want him to forget it."

"I've had Bonnie since she was three weeks old," remarked a babysitter. "I've taught her to walk and toilet-trained her and she is just like a little sister to my kids. I can't bear the thought of their moving and taking her away from me."

"I know I ought not to mind it," said a woman doctor, "but when I make all the arrangements to have my patients covered so that I can take a vacation with my family, I don't like it much when the children say they can hardly wait to get back to see if the kittens at the babysitter's have their eyes open yet."

"By Friday," says the giver, "I've got Jackie so he plays in the yard and isn't hanging around me every minute, and by Monday I have to start the whole thing over again because she never lets him out of her sight all weekend."

When users and givers are aware of their feelings, they can make an effort to deal with them realistically, recognizing that children in family day care who might otherwise live within the narrow confines of the nuclear family have the opportunity for experiencing some of the pleasure—and the pain—of children in extended families.

There are other children involved in family day care who need consideration too—those in the giver's family. Givers take on the care of another child because they want some companionship for their own young child or because, being at home with him anyway, they feel they can as easily care for two as one. If the giver's children are toddlers, they are not likely to be any happier to welcome an intruder into their domain than they are to greet a baby sister or brother. In fact, they are probably even less pleased, because it comes as a surprise. Nowadays, most parents tell their children well in advance of the birth of a new baby, but often such preparation is overlooked when "babysitting" is arranged, perhaps because the arrangement is made at short notice or because it does not seem important. Jimmy User may have learned to play with a neighbor's child quite happily and cooperatively for short periods of time, knowing he can retreat to his mother's lap if the going gets too rough. But that is very different from having an intruder in *his* house all day long, playing with *his* toys, taking up the attention of *his* mother. And, on top of it all, his mother may well insist that he shall accept the arrangement happily since if he does not, it may terminate.

School-age children may have some difficulties, too. Just because one's mother cares for a class- or age-mate, does not make him or her a friend. The best school-age care arrangements usually make it clear that the children are free to pursue their own interests, within the designated house limits, and that they need not go beyond preserving peace in their relationship with each other.

One of the greatest strains in family day care is not caused by the children but the time of day. Just when most caregivers are ready to be relieved of the care of an extra child, most small children get cross and tired. And in the homes of others, fantasies of being abandoned seem to mushroom as going-home time approaches, making children anxious and restless as well, demanding adult attention when adults are at their lowest ebb. It is unfortunate that this is often the only time when working mothers have a few minutes of their own, when they are not bound by the needs of a job or a family. It is not surprising that working women are likely to do some shopping, or have a cup of coffee with a friend, on the way to pick up their children. But if they are even a few minutes later than the agreed-on time at the giver's, the delay seems interminable to the child and to the caregiver, and friction will likely result.

Another important cause for terminating otherwise satisfactory arrangements is failure to pay promptly. The giver's irritation is not necessarily because of financial need, although that certainly enters into it. There also is the discomfort of having to remind the user of the debt which somehow makes the giver feel like a kind of beggar or servant, or a child asking for a favor rather than an independent craftsman offering something of value in exchange for cash. Like so much else in family day care, the feelings involved affect the stability of the relationship more than the reality of the situation. When a user finds herself unable to meet the financial plan agreed on, a frank discussion is much more likely to contribute to maintaining the arrangement than evading the subject.

Summary

In summary, informal day care—the care of a child of a working mother in the home of a nonrelative in an arrangement made between the two families—is so widespread that it can be called a new social custom. The most troublesome aspect for users and givers alike is finding each other and maintaining an arrangement that is positive for all concerned in both families. Good arrangements are most likely to be made between families who have compatible lifestyles and live in the same geographic neighborhood although they may not be friends (in fact, the arrangements have a better chance for success if they are not friends). Family day care arrangements will be most positive for everyone if the terms, especially in regard to payment and hours, are discussed, agreed on, and observed. The children in both families will profit from the socializing aspect of family day care if consideration is given to their stage of development. And in family day care, as in family life in general, feelings as well as facts need to be understood and dealt with by everyone. In short, family day care users and givers are engaged in a complicated, interesting, and important form of relationship which has great potential for preparing children for a future in which getting along well with other people will be an essential skill, while it also has the possibility for developing opposite kinds of attitudes, and disrupting not only the families involved but the functioning of industry, business, and the professions, which depend on the skills of working parents.

CHAPTER 2

CO-OP CHILD CARE EXCHANGES AND PLAYGROUPS

In today's lifestyles women have many interests carried on outside their own homes besides full-time employment. This has always been true of upper- and middle-class women who had servants to care for their families. Since only a very few women have full-time household help, the rest have worked out several ways of sharing child care, allowing them to pursue their interests, whether professional, political, recreational, or artistic.

Organizing Co-op Child Care Exchanges

One method is the child care exchange, whereby a group of friends and acquaintances care for each other's children through a kind of time bank. An exchange is often begun by two or three mothers living near each other who have children about the same age. One looks after the children while the other is away from home—to shop, keep doctor's or hairdresser's appointments, attend meetings or classes. The mothers make an effort to "take turns" so that no one person is always caring for the children. It often becomes clear that if there were a few more people in this mutual exchange system, every mother would have more time to follow her own interests. At this stage, one of the original "exchangers" usually takes on the task of formalizing the practice, setting up a system in which the time of each member is recorded—the hours giving care and the hours using care. It is assumed that these hours should be in balance over a given period of time—often a month. Some exchanges remain informal and the chore of keeping records up to date is taken on by one member or passed around to others. In other instances, there is a formal organization whose members vote directly for elected officers and on rules governing the exchange. Larger exchanges usually charge a small membership fee, used for maintaining necessary records. No other fees are charged. In either case, the viability and the longevity of exchanges seems to depend on the efforts of a small number of members to keep it operating on a truly reciprocal basis. Some exchanges have been self-perpetuating, recruiting new members with young children as those whose children no longer need babysitting—or who become day care givers themselves—drop out. While some exchanges attempt to involve both father and mother—for example, having one parent remain at home while the other babysits for the evening with the children of another member—this is not a common practice, and not very popular. And exchanges are not useful to full-time working mothers who cannot "put in time." On the whole, exchanges function best to meet the need most of them were organized for—to give the otherwise home-bound, child-caring mother occasional time off to use as she chooses.

A member of an exchange describes it this way:

The way it started, there were a couple of girls in the neighborhood and there weren't a lot of part-time babysitters—mostly full-time state-licensed people. So it started out with just two people exchanging and then it got bigger up to nine gals in about three months. Like, whenever someone new moved into the neighborhood, someone would have a coffee and they'd get to meet all the gals and we could decide if we wanted to invite them in—"Is this one going to fit in?"

I really don't like kids running through the house like banshees, so while Jan was a baby and Wanda took a long nap, I didn't want it—but the nice weather came and I got to know the others, so I joined.

All of us live within one mile of each other and six of us live just like around one street and the corner. I don't like night-sitting but the gals that do . . . they put the kids down in a bed—most have an extra bed and then the parents just come in and pick up their kid.

In our neighborhood we're close—some of us spend our vacations together. We don't earn alike, but all the men work for the corporation. It's right over there—you can see it . . .

Our co-op runs on an hour basis and the sort of unwritten rule is that you don't leave more than two children. This gets you to the point where you don't really get too sick of it. You can have kids from different families that way and you chalk up a lot of hours. You can't count the kids in one family as more than one but if you had three from different families, well, you chalk up three hours and you're only home that one afternoon or like that.

Our book is like a ledger. There's a page for each one—with a debit and a credit column so what you have to do is total the pages every month and balance—and that can be a bear! Everyone takes turns for two months. We all know each other—everyone does keep balanced.

I think co-ops are great because mothers can actually get away from their children, the only thing I don't like is that every time I go out I feel like I'm being punished because I know I'm going to have to take care of somebody else's kids, for my time! But it's a process of, you know, what's important to you. I have probably calmed down enough in the past two years where I can tolerate other people's children, and I've just gotten to the point where I don't let them bother me that much. I was in the hole twenty-two hours last winter, well mainly because of the neighborhood beautification committee I'm chairman of—that's taking an awful lot of my time—which chalked up the hours. They kept piling up, I kept getting deeper in, and I remember this one instance where this gal calls me, and she said, "Connie, will you babysit for me this afternoon?" And I said, "Linda, I am not fit to even care for my own children, this week, and I really feel that it would be very unfair to take yours. I really don't feel it would be fair to you or the kids. I'm in a very vile mood," I said.

But normally you don't have to give an excuse, I mean, I've called and I said, "Hey, Sue, can you babysit for me?" and she said, "Gee, I can't make it today Connie." "Okay, fine." There's a real rapport with the gals. Oh, I've gotten uptight a couple of times—asked myself, what am I in this co-op for, nobody can sit today, or when I need someone and no one can sit—but just a little thing where I'm feeling sorry for myself for being uptight.

You call and find your own sitter. You know, it's no big thing, at all. Or like when you're the secretary and someone calls you—well, who's down in hours? Then we try to use that person to build them back up so they're not so far down. Because it'll get sometimes where it is very unequally balanced, one person will have all the hours—well we don't want this—or one person will be like twenty-five hours in the hole—well hey, you know—but we never have any problems because everybody always piles back out again.

Organizing Playgroups

Playgroups have been in existence for more than twenty years in some parts of the country. Interest in them has greatly increased in recent years. Some have grown out of parent food co-ops or women's groups. They have been strong in university neighborhoods, possibly because graduate students in education and the behavioral sciences are especially interested in early childhood development and they comprise a high proportion of young families whose children have lost their former playmates in moves and need new ones.

In recent months several excellent publications have described the purpose and philosophy of playgroups and given practical advice on how to organize and run them as well as suggestions for all kinds of activities.

Playgroups–Do It Ourselves Childcare* makes this opening statement:

Do you remember what it felt like to walk down the street as fast as you wanted, to browse leisurely in a store, to read a book for an hour, do your laundry when you wanted or tackle your work for a few hours straight? Or have the diaper fumes, the toy-filled rooms, the spilled food, and two-year-old screams for attention clouded your memory of these solitary moments? Children are wonderful—but very time consuming. A parent can feel his or her own identity slipping away while catering to the needs and whims of the child.

Playgroups offer an alternative to the limitations of the nuclear family. It's not hard to form a cooperative playgroup. All it takes are some parents who enjoy working with children, some collective energy, possibly a little money from everyone, and a sense of commitment and responsibility for creating childcare that benefits both parents and children.

The concept of parent-run cooperative playgroups grew out of parents' need for inexpensive childcare and their desire to serve the needs of the parents and children. Here are some ideas and facts that we have learned from our experiences in forming our own playgroups.

If you don't already know enough people to get started, write up index cards or print up flyers about starting a playgroup, post them in laundromats, bulletin boards and your local hangouts, and then wait for the calls to come in. When you go to the park, talk to other parents there and find out if they would be interested in a playgroup....

Sizes. One of the easiest ways to get started is to form a rotating exchange among a few families (3 to 5 is about right) having the children meet in a different home, in that parent's care, each day of the week. The beauty of this arrangement is its simplicity and flexibility. Rotating exchanges don't

---

**Playgroups–Do It Ourselves Childcare* (San Francisco: Childcare Switchboard/ Single Parent Reserve Center, 1975).

require the hassle and expense of a rented place. Any household with a child will probably have all the necessary toys and equipment to take care of a few children. The familiarity of a home environment is an added security to young children. Nursing mothers may form an exchange to allow themselves a few hours of freedom. No matter what the age, children and their parents should have breathing space between each other. A rotating exchange can be an interim step in forming a co-op playgroup or an on-going daycare method.

A group of 10 to 12 children is a workable size for a more elaborate childcare arrangement. If one adult per child is responsible for childcare, a playgroup of 12 children provides 2 adults per day for each working day of the week. As more adults are involved, the ratio of free time providing child care, is increased. A group any larger than 12 can become too unwieldy to be workable and fun.

Age Range. We've found that it's best to keep the age difference around a year and a half between the oldest and the youngest children. Those too young cannot participate in all the activities of the others and frequently need special attention. Older children can get bored and impatient with the rest of the group and also require recognition of their age and abilities by the adults. Some playgroups advance the age as the children get older so members don't have to drop out because they've outgrown the group. Instead, the playgroups grow and mature as the children do.

Another new publication, *Playgroups: How to Grow Your Own,** is based on a similar philosophy and provides equally practical advice:

"Although we exchanged in five different homes, the children seemed to orient quickly to the different spaces as well as to each other and to the changing adults. At least, none of us could pinpoint any disturbances related to these changes of scene even though we had all had some questions about how our kids would adjust to them. Feelings about the group were increasingly comfortable, probably first among the children, then among the adults because of these reassuring signs."

Whichever way, most apartments and houses can accommodate four or five children pretty well after a bit of thinking and furniture moving. However it's planned, there must be a consideration of how much freedom of movement is desirable. Should the children be limited to one or two rooms, or to one floor of a house? Or should they be allowed to wander anywhere they want to? . . .

*Playgroups: How to Grow Your Own (Cambridge, Mass.: Child Care Resource Center, 1974).

It would be wise to discuss safety standards in the homes. Although it is often difficult to look around at a friend's house, no less the home of a new acquaintance and to say, "Your home is not baby-proofed enough for me," it is a lot easier to appraise these conditions at the beginning.

If you want to begin a playgroup in a non-home space, you are bound to face greater complexity. Unless the space is donated you must consider rent and other tenant responsibilities. Also, you will face questions of equipping, using, maintaining, licensing, and possibly sharing (with other after-school or evening groups). If your playgroup is starting because someone has found a suitable space already, these cautions must sound irrelevant. But it is an unnecessary pressure to decide you must find space outside your homes before the children can have a real playgroup.

All our playgroups started in homes but some have since moved to larger space and added more children. We know of others that worked out well beginning in apartment building playrooms and storefronts. If you are looking for outside space try: churches, synagogues, community centers, Y's, storefronts, private clubs, etc. . . .

Wherever you meet, whatever your flexibility, the space should be made as safe and accident proof as possible. Your activities will run more smoothly.

Staff: Do you feel the need for a coordinator or experienced person in charge?

Some of our playgroups are entirely parent exchange, where each parent takes a turn running the playgroup. This method is economical and can work well. Many parents are strongly committed to being part of a cooperative venture. For some, it is more a way to keep expenses down. However, sometimes parents prefer not to lead their playgroup alone and choose to hire someone. Others combine the two by meeting regularly with a teacher and a different parent each day. Some of our groups began as total cooperatives and hired staff as our needs or expectations changed, often continuing to put in regular hours with the children.

Obviously, one question to be answered is whether you can afford or want to pay for a hired person. We've all felt the conflict of wanting to pay decent salaries for child care to reflect our respect for this job, and feeling incapable of setting aside so much of our budgets for child care. Yet if, for example, each family pays $.75-$1.00/hour (equivalent to what one pays a babysitter) a somewhat respectable salary can be accumulated for a staff person. In addition, if people are relying on paid staff so that they in turn can work or go to school, they may have no doubts about hiring a teacher, in an effort to provide a more stable situation.

Some exchange and playgroup parents move from part-time

interests toward a full-time commitment outside the home which necessitates full-time child care and eliminates a mother's giving reciprocal care. For the most part, exchanges and playgroups have found this disruptive to the whole program. It is obvious that in a playgroup, if one of five mothers can no longer take her turn, the group must reduce its meetings to four days or enlarge to include another family. There is sometimes the question of how a working mother can compensate the others for caring for her child. The same holds true in child care exchanges. When this leads to employment of a substitute to take her place, a whole new set of relationships and roles is required. On the whole, it appears that neither of these programs is well adapted to the needs of full-time working women.

At present, both these kinds of family day care are largely organized and run by families who are not "poor" in the conventional sense of "dependent on public support," although they may have very limited funds as a result of their own choice. It would be interesting to see how these approaches could be introduced and carried forward in less privileged circumstances.

Communal Child Care

There is another type of informal child care difficult to classify because it is both care for a child in his own home and care for the child in the home of a nonrelative! A significant number of children are having this experience and many more may be involved in the future. In many communities, individuals and families are testing communal living. It could be said that, like much else in informal family day care, it is a revival of an earlier lifestyle. This is more nearly the case when a communal household consists of different generations than in those instances where a group of like-minded individuals of approximately the same age make up a common household. At first glance they may seem to resemble communities that flourished in mid-nineteenth century, but there the ideal was to share equally in the work that sustained the community as a demonstration of the "right" way in which work and its profits should be organized. Although some new communes have similar objectives, today most communal households, especially in urban areas, are chiefly a means of sharing certain lifestyles. Members typically engage in individual and different kinds of work outside the home. Communal living has advantages for people who have children and want a less confining setting than the nuclear family; for the single parent; and for those who do not have children but enjoy them; as well as for many other combinations of interests. Like playgroups and exchanges, communal living that involves children is usually the outgrowth of the interest and organization of two or three people. Contrary to the playgroups and exchanges, communal living seems well suited to the needs of working parents, since it is possible to exchange child care for evening or weekend housekeeping or other chores in a twenty-four hour arrangement. In many instances, children are considered the responsibility of all members, who care for them without the special assignment of responsibility. In other instances, there is careful assignment of all responsibilities on a permanent or rotating basis with child care as one component, or children are considered to be the sole responsibility of other members who are also parents. One does not usually find the kind of program playgroups provide, but there is a good deal of after- and before-school care that is not usually part of a playgroup program. In some instances children, even quite young, are expected to take their responsible place in the household, a custom reminiscent of an earlier time when chores were a big part of a child's life.

A graduate social work student reviewed her experiences in group living:

Actually, though this is the first time since we were married six years ago that we've lived by ourselves—my husband, my little girl, and I—I've never thought of myself as living in a commune in the way a lot of people do. It all just sort of happened logically. The first year we were married, my husband began medical school and I was finishing college so our hours never seemed to be free at the same time and we were both used to dormitory living and we simply hated our tiny apartment and the whole isolation of our lives with only each other to depend on—and not even really having that. So when a bunch of my husband's fellow graduate students found a farm to rent near town, boy, we were glad to share the rent. There was a kind of informal division—the unmarried ones lived in one of the houses on the place and we shared a little two-bedroom house there with another couple. It worked just great—someone was always around and we still had some privacy. I got pregnant and had Mimi and she was the best-observed and babysat child in the city with all those med students acting as part pros and part relatives.

So when my husband went to another city for his internship, we inquired around and found friends of friends—another resident, in fact, and they already were sharing housing with another couple with two kids, but there was room for us and we moved in. But it was murder! We thought it would be so great for our little six-month-old to share a room with the other kids, like in a big family, but the kids all kept each other awake, and we got into arguments—polite but nasty—about who should do what and a lot of the other child care things we didn't agree on. So the couple with the two kids moved out and the four of us got along wonderfully all that year.

Then, when we had to move again, they wrote some friends who were living in a big house—if there was room, and there was, and we moved in even though we didn't know them. Golly, that house was really big—nine bedrooms!—a beautiful old place, but even if we could have afforded not to fill it, being half empty made it feel sort of spooky. So gradually, we added some people who were friends of one or another of us. And we ended up with three married couples, two single women and three single men—and ours was the only child.

It worked out a lot better than everyone told us it would. We all had different kinds of professional backgrounds and jobs and we were all working, but at a lot of different hours. We worked out a careful schedule of rotating household jobs that included babysitting Mimi, which I liked a lot because it was just like being in a big family and she could be right there with her own toys, and yard, and everything.

On the whole, it worked well, we thought, until Mimi began to talk a lot about how nice "little" houses were and make us read and reread her books about the Jane and Dick type home, which we would have thought she would think was awful. And then she began to cry a lot at night and insist on me or her father coming to her instead of any of the others who used to do it if they happened to be up or hear her before we did. Then we did begin to see that though it was sort of like a big family, it really wasn't one. Everyone was darling to Mimi, but she didn't belong to them in the way she would if we were with relatives, and sometimes they'd play with her a lot and then get busy and forget about her. So we all talked it over a lot and we moved. And Mimi is really a lot happier—and I'm surprised that I don't mind it either. I'm busy now at my work; she goes to the lady next door while we're away and it seems to work out okay.

We still see our friends in the big house and it's funny; now Mimi thinks of them as her family and they are just delighted to see each other.

I couldn't really say what I think about commune living—it went fine for me and maybe it did because that was all I expected from it. I didn't see it as a new way of life, or to carry out any kind of reform. It just seemed a pleasant way of pooling the dumb housework, being with people and living in nicer places than we could possibly have afforded otherwise. I'd certainly recommend it to any young family—just so no one gets upset when it breaks up.

Experiences in community living are not confined to any social group. One single mother reports:

It's just such a hassle to find a babysitter. I'm in a training course for office-machine operator and I'm supposed to go or the caseworker gets mad, but it's so hard to find someone that is okay for Lisa. I answered an ad in the paper that said, "Loving care for your child in my Christian home" and that sounded fine and it was all right—she was loving, all right. Like, she was a grandmother and she needed the money to add to her Social Security and the house was clean and all, but mostly she just sat with Lisa on her lap, or played with her like just sitting in the yard—and she got really spoiled—no discipline at all. She thought that was what I ought to do when I got home, and, boy, after the days I have, she has to learn to be a little helpful and independent.

Then the next one was great—she potty-trained her and she said three was too old for her still to get a bottle, so she broke her of that and everything was fine there. But I had some trouble with my boyfriend and moved out, so I had to change babysitters again.

I was just about going to give up the whole training thing and go back to just being miserable in that one room when a girl in my class asked me what was wrong and I told her. And for once I lucked out—she was living in a pretty nice old house with three other girls who were divorced and had young kids and she asked me if I wanted to move in—one of the first ones had just left. So I did and it really worked out swell. She took care of all the kids in the daytime, sort of like a little school or something and the welfare paid her as an in-home caregiver. And the rest of us did the housekeeping, because she had had it by the end of the day and we thought it was okay that way. The brother of one of the girls who had custody of his little girl asked to move in and he did and it was never any trouble. We mostly each had our own boyfriends and it meant you could even get out once in a while because usually anyone who stayed home would listen for all the kids. We'd still be doing it, I guess, but the house got sold and we couldn't find another one would let us do it. One of the girls and I still room together and the kids get along really well—but we don't always! It's maybe because there's only the two of us so there's more to do and we kind of fight over it more.

As yet, it appears that there are not a great many families and children involved in any of the newly developing informal child care approaches, although such a statement can only be based on conjecture since there are no available statistics. But these are interesting new directions and offer new alternatives which may be of increasing importance in the future if funding for family day care continues to be far below the level sought by those who see it as a public responsibility toward the provision of equal opportunity for occupational choice for men and women alike.

CHAPTER 3

PUBLIC FAMILY DAY CARE

A Welfare Mother as Day Care Giver

Giver: Let me see, I have the four still—Tanya, Bobby, Herbie, and Ernie—that I had when you were here before. And then I got a little boy from the next apartment. The mother ran off and the father just didn't know what to do—the nursery said they only take them at three and potty-trained, and he sure isn't.

Interviewer: Are your reasons for babysitting still the same as when we talked before?

Giver: Well, yes, but they're changing the rules on Aid to Dependent Children, so now my babysitting money is, well, isn't extra. It's counted as part of my income so I'm not allowed to keep all of it but I'm managing to do a few extra things. I have a few goals—one of them I'll be completing the first of December. I'll have a five-hundred-dollar debt all paid off which I started last December. I'm real proud! It'll take a good chunk of December's check, but I want to pay it all off and then move to a different place and take enough kids to make it pay. I'm not sure how next year's going to go yet—in a way I'd hate to go on my own and then not have enough kids to make it pay and it's such a big thing to try to get back on Aid to Dependent Children once you're off. I'd like to have a yard for the kids and a better house and all, but I'd miss all the experiences I have here. I've been meeting a lot of people at meetings and all and I know about all my neighbors and I feel different. Before, I could just sit on the sidelines, home, but now I've intermingled and I think this is important.

Interviewer: How do you feel about babysitting?

Giver: Well, I don't mind it—I never have. I guess this is what's helped—being I have younger children, it's always worked in. I wouldn't want to take care of older children. I've always tried to keep the age of seven on down because I feel that I've got enough problems. I can't cope with my own sometimes and I don't want to take on somebody else's—and when you get older children, you do.

Interviewer: Have there been any changes in how your children feel about your babysitting?

Giver: Oh, they've always accepted it, but there are times when they'll pick on each other—they don't know why so-and-so have to be here, or why those kids have to have their way, or—I just shut my ears and go on.

Interviewer: Could you tell me something about what the daily routine is for one of the kids you take care of?

Giver: Well, like Tanya comes about ten-thirty in the morning because her mother has to be at work at eleven-fifteen. She just got a car—through a relative or friend—so she's able to get back and forth much easier. And Tanya is, oh, she's very happy here . . . and Momma comes and she's just about ready to be home with her own momma—her and Tanya's happy.

Interviewer: Do you have much chance to talk with her mother when she brings Tanya?

Giver: Well, yesterday I didn't. Today I said hello. When she brings her, she just brings her stuff and her and if there's anything for me to know, she lets me know. The lady I rent from, Carol, was upstairs and I was in the basement regulating my machine that's gone on the blink—I have to hand-work the timer—so I was just finishing a load of clothes. I didn't even know she was really here. I knew it was time, but she'd come and left when I came up, so I got Tanya some toys to play with—and she's just swell to the other children, she just joins in. She's very small yet though—of course, she's crawling. And at noon I feed the other children in the kitchen and I give Tanya half a sandwich. I put her down—well, right now, if I don't have Bobby, she goes in the playpen. Bobby's here today so I put her on the bottom bunk. I've been trying to teach her to take a nap, which she's doing right now—she's still asleep. Her and Ernie sleep on the bottom bunk and my daughter sleeps on the top to take their naps. And this varies from an hour to two hours. And she gets up and I change her—well, I change her before she goes to bed and I change her after.

Interviewer: What's she usually doing when her mother comes after her?

Giver: Well, usually, well she has supper with us and then—I try to make it a point to have the children all cleaned up and ready to go—and sometimes during the day, if they have light colored clothes on, I sometimes take the creepers off and I put on a pair of Ronnie's on her and let her crawl around and then I change her back when the mother comes so she's nice and clean. A child gets dirty—if your house is clean or not, when they crawl, they get grimy. And I thought it would help the mother a little bit. And when she comes, usually I'm entertaining them. It depends on what we're doing. Last night we just finished dinner, so my oldest boy Martin—Tanya is a big favorite of his and vice versa—and she has to sit on his lap. When Martin was little, my ex and I ran a store and Martin, he was crazy about the breadman that came every day. He was a grandfather and he enjoyed it as much as Martin did, I think—in fact, he said he did. If Martin was missing he wanted to know where Martin was, you know. But that was the real highlight of the day when the breadman came. So it's the same thing with him and Tanya. I think she misses a man—she's at this age—and she doesn't have that at home. But her mother sits and visits if she can for a few minutes, like last night she stayed and talked about forty-five minutes. Sometimes she's tired and wants to get home, but if there's no pressing hurry, we talk about Tanya. Tanya has a very bad diaper rash problem. She's allergic to herself, the clinic says, and this won't clear up until she's broke. So this is a big thing, like keeping it down. It's really impossible, but we're working on it. Even the doctor said there's nothing more we can do.

Interviewer: What other things do you talk about?

Giver: Oh, last night, a little bit of everything—we've become sort of friends in a sense. She likes to sit and visit. She has a tough time just making ends meet—she's divorced and her boyfriend has kids to support and she's got a lot of problems. Like last week she was fortunate to have a three-day holiday and she thought she would go out with her boyfriend, and they took Tanya and she had to tell me what a good time they had. I was glad even though I lost the money—she needed some fun. And we talk about everyday stuff like she wanted to know how I got my work done with all the kids around, and I told her like I just go ahead and do my housework and they can watch me if they want, or help in little ways to learn how to do things—or I do things that I can watch them while they're playing. The group I have play very well among themselves and they pick up things from each other. Like the other day Ernie, he comes after school, and he brought some Fritos or something he had left over from his lunch and he shared them with the others. I don't feel that I have to—like, this isn't a nursery school—I correct them or guide 'em, but it's not a school, it's just a home. But I guess they do learn a lot, like, I have this little playhouse with a little kitchen and I let 'em use my saucepans and spoons and other things from my drawer and I see them doing things that they've watched me do in the kitchen—and they love to be around when I make cookies.

The Evolution of Public Family Day Care

Although millions of families are involved in the kind of informal family day care described in Chapters One and Two, when family day care is mentioned, the general public—even those who have informal arrangements of their own—think first of day nurseries and then of new kinds of family day care designed to help young, disadvantaged children at the earliest possible age acquire skills they will need for later educational and vocational success. Families using this care are unable to pay for it, so it is largely subsidized by public funds and administered under agency auspices, either public or private or a combination of both.

It is not surprising that during the past ten years there has been tremendous discussion of day care for the poor since for almost the past century, it was offered only in a very limited way, largely supported without tax money. Attendance at existing nurseries did not rise, but the numbers of tax-supported women with young children did, no doubt as a result of a major social reform in the thirties which established the principle that families should be kept together, whether their parents could support them or not. It was felt that young children needed to be cared for at home by their mothers.

Eventually it seemed to many that this concept encouraged dependence, even irresponsibility. Some thought women were exploiting the Aid to Dependent Children provisions of the welfare laws—receiving additional subsistence income for each new child and avoiding either having to go to work or institutionalize the children. Men were believed to be taking less responsibility for their families' support and the "cycle of poverty" began to be discussed—with reports that many parents receiving public subsidy had been children of parents "on welfare." Lack of education as well as lack of incentive was believed to be a major stumbling block; most young families "on welfare" testified to the misery of that condition and their despair at not being able to change it for their children. While there was still a large body of opinion that viewed all dependents on public welfare as "chiselers"—parasites on society who ought simply to be cast loose to shift for themselves—the prevailing climate of the times suggested efforts be made both to help parents acquire marketable skills, making them independent of public funds, and also to provide experiences for their children, at the earliest possible age, that would prepare them to succeed educationally right from the start.

As a result of these debates—presented here in a cursory manner—there was an unprecedented allocation of money in the early sixties for day care services.

This was not the first time, however, that child care had been provided for poor working women. More than a century before, charitable middle- and upper-class people had noted that immigrant women in large cities who had the misfortune of having no one to support them and no older relatives to care for their children had to find work outside their homes and needed a safe place to leave the children during long working hours. Unless this were provided, the children would have to be left alone or in the care of a neighbor who, because she could not be paid for the care she gave, might look after them carelessly. Day nurseries were organized for these children and supported by charitable contributions, both to give children a safe, healthy environment while teaching them habits that would assure their future independence and to demonstrate to their parents how to care for future American citizens. Since many people feared that women, if permitted to do so, would prefer to join the work force rather than remain in their proper sphere—the home—staff employed by the day nurseries made sure that only the absolutely needy, whose children might otherwise be sent to institutions, were admitted.

Day nurseries were organized chiefly in urban areas. There were few efforts to provide for poor children in rural areas where both parents often worked to provide a minimal income and young children had to be left alone in the care of those too young or too old to work in the fields.

In the same period of social reform, the first formally organized agency-sponsored foster home programs developed to provide neglected children, and sometimes orphans, with substitute families who, in exchange for the child's share (or perhaps a slightly larger part) in farm and home duties, would receive a good family upbringing. As it became clear that institutions for dependent children were a poor answer to their needs, foster care programs were expanded under public support. Family foster care facilities continued to work with special small groups and populations, trying out new methods toward achieving successful development. The model that seemed most useful required well-educated staff in a high ratio of staff to children. This model was widely adopted in principle by public agencies although frequently money appropriated for the service fell short of the need in terms of staff.

Children identified by people in the community, by professionals in various disciplines, or even by their own families as needing a temporary change of home environment were referred to a trained member of the foster care staff who investigated the situation and decided whether the child would indeed profit from foster home placement, instead of institutionalization, or would remain at home with supportive assistance. If it seemed best for the child to be removed—until family difficulties could be resolved, the agency matched the needs of the foster child to what one of the foster families that had been recruited, studied, and licensed could offer him. Once placement was made, agency staff visited the foster family and the foster child regularly. The agency usually assumed both financial and legal responsibility for the foster child and closely monitored the placement. Foster parents were encouraged to discuss the child's problems and progress with the agency caseworker and sometimes training programs were instituted to upgrade foster parent performance. The degree to which this was successful depended on the quality and quantity of staff to some extent. The goal of the agency was to reunite the foster child with his family at a level of improvement that would permit them to continue normal family life. Of course, there were situations where this goal was not achieved easily or at all, and the funds that were invested in ongoing effort varied widely from place to place.

Private agencies in some cities began to see that in some families children—especially very young children—might do best if they continued to live at home and attended special programs during the day. This at first seemed suited to families with severe problems, but was then also seen as a solution for the less serious emergencies faced by families, especially single parents. The foster family day care programs administered by private agencies were usually very limited in number, but when public agencies began to subsidize family day care on a large scale, the private agency model had a major influence on the manner in which family day care administration was planned and carried out.

Public Family Day Care: Dream and Reality

It soon became clear, however, that with the numbers involved and the many changes families made in day care arrangements it would be next to impossible to follow the basic program which required making a plan for each child only after an investigation of both families by a professional worker. Caseworkers were expected to discuss the day care plan—which in many localities was of necessity in family day care settings—with the parent planning to go to work or enter vocational training. In practice, sometimes parents found their own givers and asked only to have the arrangement approved. In others, they depended for suggestions on the licensing services that grew rapidly and will be discussed in Chapter Seven.

The standard public-agency process is described in the following interview with a representative of one of the few public child care agencies able to follow the model closely.

I do initial interviews with persons wanting day care. During this interview, I determine whether the person is eligible for purchased services and together we draw up a mutual agreement for services: the client states what is needed or wanted; I state what the department can and will do. The agreement is time-limited to a maximum of six months.

In arriving at the plan for day care we discuss the various facilities in the county in relation to the child's and mother's needs. Frequently the client already has a day care plan and is just asking our department to take over payment. In other instances the client wants help in choosing an appropriate facility. The interview may also involve some counseling concerning employment or job training since these are the usual reasons for needing day care.

When an agreement is reached and the client leaves, the "behind the scenes" work begins. I clear with the day care mother or center chosen to be sure the plan is within licensing standards and the payment is acceptable. The authorization is drafted and routed to the business office. The original eventually gets to the day care provider along with billing forms and instructions.

In the meantime the case record is processed and, in most instances, is transferred back to me where it becomes part of my "ongoing" case load. If it appears the client wants or needs other kinds of help than day care, the case may be transferred to a worker in the family or children's units. Thus my name may be on the original day care authorization, but the family might at a later date have a different worker.

I handle all the "day care only" cases, but I am not the only worker handling day care. Any worker in the division of social services can authorize day care and is expected to do so when appropriate for his or her clients.

As "ongoing" worker it is my responsibility to monitor the plan, authorize changes, start and stop payment, renew agreements, and close the case when services are completed. For each of these steps I must depend on timely information from the client and/or the vendor. I am not, however, directly involved with billing and the day care payroll, which is handled by the business office.

In very few instances were funds available to make it possible for agencies to follow the model considered most effective—the careful investigation and matching of both families and ongoing close professional service. It must be said that that model was, even in foster care, more honored in the breach than in the observance, but it did firmly remain the philosophical base for agency family day care. There was a general conviction that the decision to place the child, to decide on the best situation for him, and to supervise care received constituted "quality" day care—in contrast with the informal system, termed "custodial" family day care, where this degree of control did not prevail.

The objective—to make parents independent of public support and prepare children to take full advantage of future education—influenced the programs also. Day care itself became a training program for women who could then go into it as day nursery staff or perhaps as directors of family day care in home mini-centers.

The program in one large city is described as follows:

> Historically, Family Day Care has developed from two sources. In 1964, the Office of Child Welfare of the Department of Social Services perceived care provided in a safe and stable home setting as a protective and preventive means by which to obviate the need for foster care. Thus, "the cluster home" concept came into being, with each such cluster assigned as a case load to central Office of Child Welfare staff for supervision and monitoring.
>
> In 1967, the Career Program was launched by the Development Agency to provide "Work Opportunities and Incentives for Independence" to families receiving public assistance. Mothers who received Aid to Dependent Children (A.D.C) were offered the opportunity to enroll in training programs leading to full-time jobs as Career Mothers, or, in the alternative, to become Provider Mothers and care for the children of those Career Mothers.

There were a large number of training programs for family day care givers, some of which are described in some detail in Chapter Eight.

Under some programs, family day care developed as part of a "system." This was usually a central core of professional people trained in early-childhood education, health, safety and in counseling skills whose administrative function was described in one state as "including, but not limited to, training of operators of day care homes, technical assistance, and consultation to operators of family day care homes; inspection, supervision, monitoring and evaluation of family day care homes, referral of children to available health and social services."

A number of such systems also included, or were in fact centered in, a day nursery which shared the expert professional staff. Few public agencies actually administered these "satellites" themselves, but rather funded private agencies that had already had some experience in providing services of various kinds to families and children. In some imaginative "systems," family day care givers made use of the day nursery for a part of the day, thus providing a group experience for the children they usually cared for in their homes. At the same time the family day care givers also had an opportunity to observe the children in groups and were able to use the advice and methods of the group program leaders in their home-based care.

In a few instances where the two services existed, it was assumed that family day care was only offered for children too young to enter the day nursery or, as one critic put it: "One of the objections to the satellite system is that I see the center using the day care home as a dumping ground—any child that doesn't fit in is put in a day care home as though that's the place you go when you can't make it in a center, and others get moved into the center at three whether their parents want it, or they don't."

At least one private agency has successfully established a family day care program in a public housing project, no small achievement simply in terms of the financial red tape involved.

To get more money through the public title funds, we decided to locate the bulk of our new family homes in public housing where most of the families would meet the necessary eligibility requirements. They had to be low-income and those on public assistance had priority. Also, we wanted to counteract some of the problems in family day care we had noted in other services like inconsistency of care if the family day care giver got sick. So we wanted to locate groups of four to six homes within easy walking distance and develop systems among those givers so that they could take on each other's kids in an emergency. That way, everyone being close together and probably already knowing each other, we thought it would be easiest on the kids and it would also enable us to give the day care givers' vacations and holidays without upsetting the kids' or their parents' arrangements. We used our professional staff—social workers—to recruit the givers and to make decisions about how many kids we might place there—some could do fine if they only had one, others could handle up to four.

Once they're approved, we guarantee them twenty dollars a week whether or not they have kids—just like we pay our typists even if there is a slow day and we haven't much work for them to do—but we pretty much always have plenty to keep the givers busy. We were fortunate that we could persuade both the Children's Division not to deduct their earnings from their stipends and the Housing Authority not to raise their rent or put them out if they earned a little money in family day care. We're located in an area of a lot of different immigrant groups and we have a lot of parties in the building for the givers and the users, too. The social workers visit the givers regularly, but they try not to interfere too much with the ethnic customs of both families.

As more and more experience has been gained all over the country, many public agencies have modified the original models. One official commented:

Staff no longer see family day care as an offshoot of foster care. We used to, but there are many differences so we don't operate just that way any more. There is much more service to mothers about day care on the part of caseworkers. I've been doing day care reviews, which means I read records and work with county staff to see what's happening. I'm really impressed with the comfortable feelings staff seem to have developed with talking to mothers about day care and the response of the mothers. They phone all the time and say things like, "I'm considering trying to put the kids in care and going to work—what do you think?" Or, "Something's happening at the babysitter's I'd like to talk to you privately about." Or, "My babysitting arrangement has fallen through—do you think it's my fault and I should just give up trying to go on with this training?"

It used to be when we started that we'd have a mother go into training and the provider changed every week. But now it's a lot better—the staff has helped the providers know what to expect and we have a lot more good ones now.

And then I think the county administrators are really getting to see the program as useful, not just one more thing that's been laid on them when they're already too busy to breathe.

People giving day care who are on assistance are working out fine—really good success. We advance them some money to get started and the staff have been pretty ingenious about getting people to come talk to them on various things like the college extension agent. We're really holding on to a lot of them and they're liking the work.

One can predict that as experience is gained and exchanged all over the country, public agencies will continue to experiment with other ways of delivering family day care services, perhaps borrowing some ideas from the informal field, too. What is harder to predict, unfortunately, is what funding will be available to allow not only for future development but even for maintenance of present programs.

As this is written, the crystal ball is rather cloudy, but priorities do change over time with changing economic conditions and political realities and there is a growing national concern for the welfare of children all over the country that may now, as it has before, influence the allocation of government funds to human services.

CHAPTER 4

INFORMATION AND REFERRAL SERVICES

Building a Bridge for Users and Givers

Uncertainty about the level and duration of public funding for day care has always been disheartening to those who view it as one of the most effective forms of preventive intervention at every level. And it has often seemed to champions of day care support that they were spending a disproportionate amount of time lobbying for funds when there was so much more direct, interesting, and rewarding work to be done. But, in proverbial fashion, there have been some bright rays of light in the dark, foreboding clouds.

The coalitions of family day care advocates that developed in the face of threats to its support demonstrated that day care was no longer an issue only as it related to the "poor." In fact, definitions of "poverty" had little meaning in discussing day care services. A "middle-class" suburban divorcee with a college education might be poor because she had no marketable skills to contribute to the support of her young children while an intact, if not legally sanctioned, family of craftsmen might make playgroup arrangements that gave their children and those of their friends a richer experience than could be found in more formal programs. It has become increasingly clear that since family day care is today a part of the life of all the children in a neighborhood, it will serve them best when their parents and friends work together to make the best use of what is available and develop and test out new ways of increasing the quality and quantity of the care they want. Three recent developments will be discussed in this section; all rely on the cooperative efforts of those in the formal and informal family day care field.

This chapter describes information and referral services, given priority here because it has high priority for users, givers, and professionals and because, since some information and referral goes on in most communities, steps toward expansion are relatively quick and not too difficult.

We noted in previous chapters that users and givers are constantly in search of each other, a search likely to be more urgent for users than givers. But even if the pressure is less for givers, it is still frustrating to want to give care to add to family income while remaining at home, to know there are many people looking for such care, and yet lack the bridge to facilitate their meeting.

Some bridges do already exist, or at least there are structures in use, though this may not be their prime purpose. License bureaus fall in this category. They are most likely tax-supported, serving a large, legally defined territory, and housed in a public child welfare department, though they may also be found in a health or fire department. Their task, in general, is to assure that the public is offered services in an environment that is safe, healthy, and meets the given licensing standards. Licensing for certain kinds of day care has for some time been considered essential.

Most licensing departments have staff that inspect day care centers and issue operating permits, although the exact definition of what constitutes a center may vary, from a place for ten children to one with more than one hundred cared for up to ten hours a day. Until recently licenses were not required for people giving family care in their own homes. Today, however, when much money is federally reimbursable only to licensed facilities, many more licensing bureaus have taken on responsibility for licensure of family day care. The problems this has raised will be discussed in Chapter Seven. Here, it is important to note that license bureaus naturally accumulate files of names of family day care licensees which they make available to the public as a service, with the hope that it will contribute to improved child care.

While this process was not entirely successful, either in eliminating poor day care or assuring excellent care in every licensed home, the lists were consulted by many people. Unfortunately, few licensing bureaus were able to advise callers about anything more than whether a giver was licensed or not. This information was often less than callers wanted. They wanted to know something about the personal characteristics of the caregiver, a matter of crucial importance in making an arrangement that would be comfortable for the child and meet his parents' standards. The head of a day care service for families receiving public support said:

> It's not unusual for us to get calls from Mrs. X saying, "I just came here and my children used to be in day care and I want to find a place for them here so I can go to work. Can you suggest . . .?" They don't want to use our licensed homes, they couldn't anyway because they are just for our clientele and there are also residency requirements—but they want some verification that the family they leave their child with would be okay. If we happen to know a home—it would probably be a home that recently closed with us for whatever reason—sometimes we can suggest that, but we don't like to do even that because if things wouldn't be the way they wanted . . .

On the other hand, givers calling for names of people looking for care often could not be given such information, but were usually advised that if they became licensed, their names would go on the list and they could then make their own judgments about users who would call them directly. While licensing services performed useful functions, they left much to be desired for users and givers in urgent need of that bridge.

Employment offices received a few calls, but rarely accepted them, since they had no procedures for registering day care givers or were unable to attract individuals paid at such a low scale. The calls were often from employers of users who wanted to avoid losing a valuable secretary because she had to stay home and care for a child.

Social Security offices and services to the elderly were also frequently asked for names of individuals who might want to do "babysitting" either in "exchange for a good home" or on a daily basis. Social Security offices are not permitted by law to give out any information about recipients, even if they could have answered such inquiries from information on file. And although child care has long been part of grandmotherly tradition, in fact there were never many people known to services for the aged who wanted to do this kind of work, and perhaps even fewer well suited to its strenuous requirements.

Day care centers, public and private, received many requests for help in finding family day care for children whose needs did not fit their time and age boundaries. Some centers were staffed with social workers who could give some general advice and make referrals, but few were able to do it as adequately as they would have liked since these conversations were usually a time-consuming addition to already heavy duties.

In a few instances, special information and referral services were set up through a central association of day care services—those affiliated with a United Fund or Day Care Council. Here, trained staff welcomed calls from givers, users, job-seekers, employers, or anyone else in the community with some special interest in day care.

A few day care centers, mainly those organized to provide care to a certain geographic area—as in the many Model Cities programs—also had information service and could make referrals to both users and givers in the particular locale. They might be able to direct a caller to a similar community service in the caller's neighborhood, but these services were so ephemeral in many instances that they hesitated to refer people hard-pressed for time to another agency that might already be nonexistent, have rules different from their own, or offer contradictory advice. For both users and givers it was often nightmarish, having to make a number of calls to different agencies, explain their circumstances and needs to each, and then to get no response or conflicting advice.

Informal Information and Referral

With the pressure of demand, another kind of information service has emerged, largely within the informal family day care field, and is, as might be expected, a formalization of the early way users and givers had found each other. In the extended family, or the close-knit rural neighborhood, word of mouth would often supply what was needed almost before individuals recognized the need! Aunt Jane would appear to take the children to her house for the day if the grain was obviously ripe for cutting and their mother certain to have a large number of big meals to get. If a breadwinner died, or became incapacitated, the whole extended family might discuss how the children could be best cared for and perhaps offer a choice or "take turns." Somehow, usually one member of the family took the initiative for organizing these plans. Her descendants nowadays seem to do much the same thing, often for strangers as well as for friends.

Everyone knows some person who can be counted on to make useful suggestions about givers and users and also to know where to send those she personally can't help. A supervising bank teller on leave while staying home with her own small children said:

I just sort of drifted into all this matching up. I seem to get a lot of phone calls from mothers who called someone I know and they told them to call me. I try to match them up if I can, but I'm not always that successful. What gets me is when they thank me a lot even when I haven't done anything! One mother said, "I'm so sick of getting turned down and not finding a good babysitter, I think I'll just quit working and babysit instead. Can you tell me what I have to do to get licensed?" I was glad I could do that, anyway.

Another one called and she said, "It's so frustrating. I'm single and I have to get jobs I can do—cocktail waitressing or working in a department store—and no one wants a kid around after five o'clock. They say their husbands don't like it. Well, my kid is only six and I can't leave him home alone, so what am I going to do?" And here I am, trying to give her some advice like finding someone in the nursing school for instance; and there my baby is sitting on the floor next to me playing with the carving knife, and Sam has just run out the door without any clothes on and my relatives are coming for dinner and I am trying to make a fancy dessert . . .

Sometimes it's really ridiculous and I think how nice and peaceful it used to be just working eight hours a day at the bank! But then . . .

Some people find themselves looking for a way of continuing to be helpful without having to spend all their time at the corner of the kitchen table with piles of notes and telephone in hand. Eventually some of these "kitchen corners" get overcrowded and friends band together to find more adequate quarters to house them and perhaps some like-minded friends to volunteer a few hours a week and add some telephones. This has been successfully, if not easily, done in several instances.

Some, by virtue of their sponsorship or their own backgrounds, specialized in helping certain kinds of people—the students at the university or members of women's organizations. But while they may have started there, soon many were giving information to any caller who asked for it, perhaps going on to develop special publications or special services based on the very considerable skills and talents of volunteers they attracted. When they could not help, they usually made an effort to be knowledgeable about other possible resources and refer callers to them.

In its newsletter one service describes its origin and expansion:

The Pre-School Association of the East City is an instance of a typically local phenomenon: when citizen-residents discover that no one is doing a certain kind of job, they band together and organize to get it done. In this case, the situation in 1969 was that all the different kinds of early childhood education programs in the East City—nursery schools, day care centers, Head Starts, and so on—related to different offices of the city for licensing, funding and/or administration, and there was no place for exchange of information and support on a neighborhood basis.

From this recognition came a new sort of organization, the Pre-School Association, which is a means of communication among the neighborhood's great variety of settings where young children are cared for. Early on, it became a source of information for parents seeking a children's program appropriate to the age of their child, to the family's schedule and to their pocketbook. The existence of the Association has aided schools and centers to experiment in new funding arrangements for child care.

Part of the communication is via the *Newsletter*, which has come to be appreciated among those in East City and elsewhere in the city who need to be up to date and well informed on what is happening in child care.

Another information and referral service, formed with a special clientele in mind—single parents, now offers:

Childcare referrals of all sorts, including public, private, cooperative, and babysitting. Shared housing referrals, mainly for single parents. General support for single parents including rap groups, and health, legal, and welfare referrals. Family Day Care training and support. Play group/cooperative childcare set-up and support. Toy lending library, and toy and supply coop. Bi-monthly newsletter.

Paradoxically, the more successful these independent services become, the more strained are their facilities in terms of space, telephone, personnel and the ability to keep up with the collection of information. This leads to a search for funds to support expansion, a time-consuming and discouraging use of leaders who may or may not possess great talent for public relations but are interested chiefly in providing increasingly useful service. It soon becomes clear, too, that expansion in a very short time leads to increased demand, again outstripping ability to respond as word of mouth spreads about the excellence of the informal information and referral service and its friendly interest in the problems of its callers.

Public, specialized information and referral services face much the same problem except that they are often prevented from expanding by the terms of their funding sources. They, too, see unmet need and even overmet need—that is, they have more personnel to service their specific clientele than they can make use of effectively and are prevented from accepting calls from people they would like to serve but are not eligible. In the face of declining funds and increased demand, some communities are recognizing that a comprehensive information and referral service, consolidating those already in existence under one roof and acting as a kind of supermarket for direction to service and a clearinghouse for referral, will give a community high return for relatively little investment. It can help satisfy the goal of all involved in day care—the integration of this new social custom into the entire community.

Developing a Comprehensive Service

The trend toward establishing comprehensive information and referral services to meet the needs of many different groups of people is also developing rapidly throughout the country. (The government public action pamphlet, *Information-Giving and Referral*, DHEW Publication Number OHO 175-20112, offers an excellent model for such an ambitious undertaking.) Here we will describe only a possible model for a day care information and referral service which could be quite quickly activated in any community. If it then seems desirable to become a component of a larger service making use of recording and retrieval systems of greater sophistication, this will be easily accomplished.

What is not usually easily accomplished is the step that must precede the organization of even a modest consolidation of service—the convening of all existing services in order to plan together for a simple one that, while it will certainly lessen agency autonomy, will gain by pooling information and supplying one central location which can answer day care questions and make referrals with maximum efficiency and minimum waste of time.

Agencies may initially be reluctant to share information in their files, since some of it is seen as confidential, but this material really is not, for most callers have had to contact a number of these agencies, supplying each with the same information, making it no longer confidential in the usual clinical sense. Once consolidation is decided upon, the location and design of space to be used is a less sensitive matter, but an important one. In our experience it is best to locate the information and referral service where it is not strongly identified with an agency or a special population, such as a church. Its title or answering service should not imply that it "belongs" to any special group, but is rather a service for the public, similar to a library information department.

It is desirable to house the staff in one large room, together with files of resource materials. In this way, information can quickly and easily be interchanged, even while a client is waiting on the telephone. By overhearing each other, both volunteer and professional staff improve their techniques.

At the outset, a staff should include a director with a professional social-work degree and considerable administrative experience. The director will be responsible for making the basic decisions about the distribution of work and evaluating its effectiveness. The director will assist staff in using the telephone as a service tool and sensitize staff to those situations which might best be turned over for advice to the director. Volunteers and staff should have the same status except for hours of work. The director will communicate with referral sources and be responsible for formal efforts to bring the service to the attention of the public.

An information and referral service might start with a paid staff of three or four persons without specific training credentials but with an ability to respond in a friendly, helpful manner without becoming personally involved. Willingness to accept the discipline of record-keeping is essential, too, and should be explored with applicants for the job, who may not find this compatible if not forewarned. When the service has been in operation for six months, there should be a review participated in by staff, volunteers, and of course the director. If the information and referral service is a success, a perennial subject for discussion will be the constant rise in demand. Experience suggests the remedy most often proposed is employment of additional staff. This should be resisted until other alternatives using existing staff are explored. Resistance to such suggestions may well signal that staff is bored or dissatisfied with the task. This may not be the real source of discomfort; for the first time, staff may have come into direct contact with the difficulties inherent in day care and developed the "you-can't-get-there-from-here" syndrome! Skillful leadership can convert this doubt into pleasure in the variety of problems and challenge the work offers and a realistic acceptance that no agency can hope to solve all the problems it would like to.

The service should collect and disseminate specific information such as names of givers and users in family day care; of day care centers and their eligibility rules (ideally, it would be a service to centers and callers alike if the information and referral service could keep up to date on which have openings and which do not); on playgroups and other informal cooperative day care organizations. Keep current information on associations and training courses, as well as openings for staff in day care facilities. It goes without saying that information and referral services should know the restrictions or regulations affecting day care, such as licensing, and be prepared to interpret them so they are seen as protection rather than unreasonable restriction on freedom of choice.

An information and referral service will quickly find itself in the same bind it was organized to avoid if it views itself as an advisory or advocacy service, since this would require a trained staff far beyond the limits of possibility. There should be a firm commitment to providing information on the telephone, which might include brief counseling, if requested, about a day care or other problem but not attempt the kind of in-depth relationship a caller may need to resolve the problem. Referral to an appropriate agency and every possible means of effecting such a referral, not the solution of the problem, is the responsibility of an information and referral service.

The information and referral service's greatest contribution to advocacy is its unique capacity for providing accurate information about services and needs. Here, too, it should keep current information on individuals and organizations who have taken on advocacy responsibilities. The services outlined here may seem a disappointingly narrow goal for an information and referral service, but it is in fact an extremely broad one not now undertaken by any other agency in most communities.

If the information and referral service operates effectively as sketched above, some additional important needs will be met, which are less apparent than that of users seeking givers and vice versa. The chance to collect accurate information about need through maintaining records is not to be belittled. Many communities have had the disappointing experience of conducting an expensive survey of need of day care service and organizing the wanted services, only to find them underused. In a field so marked by mobility it is inevitable that respondents who once said they would be delighted to use a day care facility if it existed may have long since made other arrangements or moved away by the time the service is provided. Information and referral services provide current information, not only about what new services may be needed but what existing services might do to change their procedures, perhaps only slightly, to meet a need they were not aware of. The information and referral service can—and undoubtedly will—keep the community informed about need while pointing the way to more effective use of money already committed.

Satellite Information and Referral Services

It is undeniable, however, that if the public relations of the information and referral service are as good and pervasive as they must be, the demand for service will grow, at least for the foreseeable future. Expansion of service without adding staff can be done by developing a series of informal satellite information and referral services using individuals described as Day Care Neighbors in Chapter Six.

One information and referral service worker reports:

I noticed that a Mrs. Parker called us several times, but that from the record it didn't look as though she wanted anything for herself. Once she said she had been looking after a couple of small children for a medical student family and now they were moving to another part of the city for his internship and could we supply the names of good babysitters there for the mother to go see? Mrs. Parker explained that she wanted to help out by getting a few names and thereby saving these busy young parents some time. She could tell the people we might know about the children and so on and then the family could just have to contact those few who seemed to fit in. Then, the next time her name was listed it was as the source for a prospective giver who called and said Mrs. Parker had told her we were nice and could maybe help her find the kind of kid she wanted to take care of; or did we think she ought to take some courses and go into preschool teaching instead; and what was there?

Well, so then we had one of those things that happen and you always wish they wouldn't. A lady called to say the giver we had told her about was a dirty, neglecting woman and how dare we ... and so on. It scares you to death though it doesn't happen often and we *always* tell everyone they have to make their own decisions about the people—all we have here are names, and whether or not they are licensed. Well, we keep notes on everyone referred and the notes on the giver were all pretty complimentary, but still we didn't want to go on giving out her name after that report—only was it true? So Jo thought of calling Mrs. Parker, who lives a block away from the lady who was supposed to be so bad, and of course not telling her the story, but just kind of asking for a reference, like. And she was great and told us she knew the lady and was sure she was wonderful with kids, but she wasn't much of a housekeeper. So after that we used to call Mrs. Parker quite often and she called us and we got to see we were using her as a sort of annex!

There are several ways in which information and referral services can make excellent use of people like Mrs. Parker, and others will no doubt be discovered. The service might employ a social worker whose job includes consultation with those who present themselves as neighborhood resources, or with Day Care Neighbors, and with those in neighborhoods that the information and referral service records show to be underserved or underused, providing the social worker with some variety in professional activity which may be welcomed. Other staff members who ordinarily do not go out of the office may be trained as consultants. In any case, the partnership of a number of Day Care Neighbors will greatly increase the range and volume of service for the information and referral service at the lowest cost, eliminating the need for extra space, more telephone service and other overhead as well as staff expansion.

An information and referral service can also conserve staff, increase its visibility, and offer better service by making extensive use of volunteers who wish to remain in touch with helping services without taking on responsibility that's incompatible with their private lives but is more demanding than stuffing envelopes. The brief contacts in an information and referral service permit volunteers to serve in the same capacity as other staff in contrast to some settings where ongoing relationships must be maintained by professional staff. Training is not extensive if volunteers are well screened initially for their ability to be friendly and make quick and accurate responses or referrals. Their time can be flexible and their understanding of community needs enormously expanded. They also contribute to the service through feedback they bring from the community.

A final word should be said about records. They must be viewed not as a necessary nuisance but as the lifeblood of the agency and its lifeline for continued community support. They should be well designed, preferably with expert assistance, initially. Where computerization is possible, now or in the future, they should be designed so this transition will be easy. Every call, no matter how irrelevant, should be recorded, if only with a note, saying "unintelligible call" or "caller wanted day care for mental patient." Each card should at a minimum have the address of the caller.

Most callers will volunteer information about what they want, generally and specifically, and there should be room on the record card for this information but it should not be elicited in a filling-out-every-box manner. Avoid any intimation of a means test or court procedure, which may distress callers who have had unfortunate contacts with this kind of probing. Codes denoting remarks by the interviewer or others in firsthand contact should be used if practical, but space for longer notes is desirable, too, even if it cannot be provided on the same record card, and has to be recorded in a special notebook or file.

Referral information, too, should be carefully recorded. It is useful to assign certain kinds of data collection to specific staff members who are responsible for keeping it up to date and maintaining the kind of liaison with the information source that will make for easy and successful referral and other transactions.

Although this account may make an information and referral service sound like a complex, burdensome undertaking, it will not prove to be so, since it will probably start fairly modestly and grow as staff skills improve.

CHAPTER 5

ASSOCIATIONS:
FAMILY DAY CARE GIVERS ORGANIZE

How Associations Developed

Although there have been Associations of day care givers in some cities for many years, the strong movement throughout the country toward their formation began only recently. In fact, they have developed so rapidly it is not possible to describe them with detachment or make valid predictions about their future. It seems clear, however, that Associations are growing in response to a felt need of their members and they will influence the direction of family day care and day care agencies in important ways in the future.

Like so much else in day care, Associations began in different ways, but probably the most pervasive influence was attendance at mandatory agency training courses for present and prospective day care givers. Here, in discussions during and after the formal training program, day care givers found they had many common interests, problems, and frustrations. They wanted to go on meeting with each other and talking about them. At the least, these meetings helped offset the isolation experienced by any woman homebound with young children. At best, they helped day care givers see agency personnel in a helping light, even as "being on their side," when previously they may have been viewed as punitive snoops. Staff, too, often saw possibilities of enlarging the purpose of the training programs.

In other instances, energetic day care givers spontaneously convened others so their combined efforts might bring results they could not achieve singly. What to do about liability insurance; low rates of pay, often officially set; the intricacies of income taxes; and what to do when children and their parents presented problems day care givers could not solve but knew were serious? Givers held meetings and sometimes developed a newsletter or bulletin to reach members and prospective members.

Encouragement for Associations came from another corner—the somewhat unexpected one of licensing personnel, reminded daily of the magnitude of their task and their inability to meet its demands. Charged not only with inspection of day care givers to see if they could be licensed but also with the task of bringing them up to standard and helping them improve practice, some perceptive licensors recognized the potential help day care givers themselves could give. They might then encourage forming groups of day care givers around one or two able individuals, remaining in contact with them minimally on specific request.

The licensing director of a large city public day care agency said:

When I got into it, it was mainly a licensing function—teaching givers what they had to do to get licensed—but then I began to see what an Association could do for them. It's not our function officially to get involved and it isn't now connected to us officially, but we've given support to it. In some places you find that Associations are set up because of the problems of the givers with the agency and it's a "for" and "against" thing. I just say the idea of getting our agency starting, it was a matter of saying we can't handle it—aren't staffed to meet all their needs and the day care givers are capable of handling their own needs if they have some support! They do a lot.

What Associations Can Do

A major unifying force in the life of Associations was lively discussion of rules being promulgated to govern family day care, an issue that burst into flame when large sums of public money were invested in day care services. As has been noted, a small number of agency-affiliated day care givers had previously been subsidized by the supervising agencies, which had selected them in accordance with their own standards of excellence. In nonsubsidized private family day care, arrangements were made between users and givers to their mutual satisfaction. Very few localities required conformity to an official set of standards for family day care givers caring for a small number of children, and even fewer made an effort to enforce existing regulations. If day care givers who had formerly been caring for children without restriction were to do so for the children of mothers being urged to acquire skills toward financial independence, they would have to be licensed in conformity to regulations promulgated by the official public agency, which, in turn, was governed by state and federal rules.

In most instances, these regulations derived from those already in force in most communities for group day care facilities and set physical requirements that often were entirely irrelevant to family day care. What upset day care givers even more were the attitudes implied in regulations toward givers. It seemed the value of their relationships with the children was so denigrated that the quality of the relationship was not even mentioned as a criterion, although details of household arrangements were minutely spelled out. Or the rules reflected the old view of day care givers as drunken, neglecting neighbors who were to be controlled by inspection of facilities, judgments about worthiness, and ongoing supervision. And finally, pay rates were usually set at the bottom of the scale already in effect in the community, reflecting once again the public view of the unskilled and low status of family day care.

It was not surprising that one of the liveliest topics discussed in the first Associations were these new regulations. Associations, with and without staff encouragement, found courage to make their voices heard in public on these issues. In some instances, day care givers could be more convincing advocates than public agency staff, who might encourage their activity while remaining out of the limelight.

Associations did not find fuel for action only in broad issues. They gave common voice to grievances individual members would have hesitated to express.

An Association chairman said:

The Day Care Mothers Association set up meetings with the licensing staff because some of the day care mothers are very uptight about licensing. It seems like some of the caseworkers really don't have any idea what family day care is about. We set up this idea of having them leave a copy of what they write on their licensing form for the day care mother to read so there is some kind of common ground for the two of them to talk about. The day care mother felt so sort of intimidated—the caseworker would be writing it all down and leave and the day care mother would wonder, "Wow, what does she think of me? What did she think of my bathroom?" and all that stuff. Like, one of our more active members—she takes courses, and she comes to all our meetings, and she reads a lot—but in the space on the form that said, "Does this woman do any extracurricular activities to enhance her home?" the caseworker had left it blank. She didn't even realize what it meant!"

We're asking for in-service training for the caseworkers that do the licensing, and we want to be a part of it. We'd like each one to spend a day in a day care home. At one of our last meetings with the supervisors we've been talking to, she said, "We realize you have needs and we have just hired a nutritionist to work with you." And we go, "Groan—what do we need with a nutritionist?" Every place you look there is free advice about what to feed kids—and we've all fed our own families.

Whether their large or small campaigns were successful or not, the experience of joining together on an issue and taking action often worked as a unifying force, stimulating the development of Associations, giving them focus and direction. There was, however, the danger that once the unifying issue was settled one way or another, the Association might become passive and fall apart. This was undoubtedly the fate of some with strong outside direction targeted toward a single issue. But others went on in directions of special interest to their members—general child advocacy, for example; promoting a better self-image for family day care, and many others.

A county Family Day Care Center Association listed the following as some of its activities for 1973-74:

- With the help of the Social Services, obtained an increase in rates for welfare recipient children.
- Worked with the University to solve problems of use of space and equipment in day care homes.
- Represented day care homes on a committee for the Task Force on Women and Child Care.
- Represented day care homes as guest speakers at meetings of other community organizations.
- Shared our ideas with new day care organizations statewide.
- Participated in a day care homes course offered by the public schools.

- Spoke on different areas concerning day care at the State Family Day Care Association convention.
- Represented day care on the advisory committee to Social Services and steering committee to State Public Welfare.
- Facilitated day care homes' access to social services and mental health center for help for themselves, the children, and their families.
- Printed a guide to selecting day care homes.
- Wrote to newspapers and legislators about quality child care.
- Collected and offered day care mothers inexpensive and free materials, built up a library.
- Organized a clothing bank.
- Held workshops and meetings on fire safety, children with attachment problems, introduction to the Social Services Department child care, licensing of day care homes, income taxes, and rap sessions.
- Sent out a newsletter.

The first active Associations provided models for other groups to follow. At a statewide meeting of Associations, a member from a rural county said:

I work as treasurer of our town Association and I'm in touch with a lot of day care mothers. Just in this little place there's about thirty new mothers giving care every month and about twenty-five mothers quit. That's a pretty big turnover. I think a lot of it is frustration—not knowing how to run a business and handle problems with parents. Our Association is only four months old, but we are trying to contact all the newly licensed day care mothers through our newsletter and through personal phone calls and we say if they have questions or a problem, to call one of us who's been doing it long enough that we might be able to help them.

It was my idea to have an Association—I heard about the one in the city and I thought we ought to have one, so a couple of us got together and said, "Okay, who'll take what jobs?" We needed it, for one thing, to work with the welfare department—we only get three dollars a day and they don't want to listen to individuals—it takes numbers. So now at least we got a little raise, but we'll get more if we find out what other places pay, and what our costs are. Maybe it will be still hard, but they didn't listen to us at all when we asked just as individuals.

I've done a lot of reading and I'd like to see a lot of things happening in day care, on the local level but state and federal, too. My husband's union is interested in day care—one of their locals funded a day care center, with satellite day care homes.

It should be noted that even with excellent staff leadership, promoting the formation of even a small Association is not easy. A social worker with much experience in community action was asked to lead a group of family day care givers living in public housing and subsidized by a private day care agency:

We brought them together for a series of evening meetings on child care with the objective of getting them to decide what they wanted to know more about and, hopefully, to form themselves into an organization which could take over training, represent their groups and the families they cared for in public, and so on. I used the kinds of approaches I had often done pretty successfully in other groups but I drew a blank—and I mean blank. They just sat and looked at me and made it plain that even if I was black and they were black, they couldn't care less about what was going on and they were only there because they had to be. So I got pretty upset and fell back on following the county family day care training manual I'd been given, which I hadn't planned to do. But that too, was a resounding failure. They made it clear to me that all I was going to get was their physical presence because that was required. It was pretty discouraging to me because I have done a lot of work in community action and I have never before found myself so shut out by a group that seemed so apathetic.

So I fell back on the training manual and talked about what children need and so on. It was Spring and I tied the exploration of the environment to the possibility of taking all the children on a trip to a nearby park. The whole group suddenly came to life and one of them said, "Yeah, why don't we go to the park? I've never been—my mother was always too busy to take us. Let's us go next week instead of coming here." Before I really knew it, they had organized an outing, not for the children, but for themselves. Several mothers planned times, transportation, even what food to take, and all I did was agree that it could be done instead of the training session scheduled. And it was amazing to me—those young women had such a good time on the swings and just sort of acting like kids.

After that, there was no more problem with the course. They continued an informal organization—they never did officially elect officers—and followed the pattern that first outing set. First they would do something and then they would plan it for the kids they were taking care of and their own kids. I learned to keep my program very practical and not to try to get them to go to the legislature and that sort of thing that community action groups wanted to do. Maybe some day—but for now they are what they say they are, The Hillside Apartments Day Care Club.

A project with the major objective of helping family day care givers enhance their image has had a profound effect on the rapid development of Family Day Care Associations throughout the country. It has been excellently described by the project director, June Solnit Sale, quoted in part here:

A Profile of WATCH
(Women Attentive to Children's Happiness) *

The Community Family Day Care Project was initiated in August 1970 by Pacific Oaks College in order to examine family day care and its potential for delivering developmental services for young children. What we found, we liked. We as a staff also found ourselves becoming family day care advocates, not objective researchers but defenders of women who were providing services that in no way reflected the pitifully small monetary rewards they were receiving.... As we traveled, communicated with, and met family day care mothers in other communities, we became more convinced that women like the women with whom we worked might be found in any neighborhood. It became clear to us that the family day care mothers themselves could best dispel the myths spread about them. They had to become more visible.

The Community Family Day Care Project provided the opportunity for bringing small groups of family day care mothers together for the purpose of discussing strengths and weaknesses of this type of child care. The act of bringing 5 or 6 women together in the Project Office resulted in other informal get-togethers, pooling of resources, exchanging of equipment, helping with vacation times and lots of telephone calls outside the program. During this time, the staff and Pacific Oaks students observed an improvement in the self-image of the women and the quality of programs offered parents and their children. Indeed, the family day care mothers wanted more than their own small group meeting; they wanted the opportunity to meet the total membership of the Project, to meet as a whole. They wanted to compare notes, find more friends, assist each other and learn ways of coping with common problem situations. The staff quickly recognized that the women themselves could and would often provide assistance most

---

*"A Self-Help Organization of Family Day Care Mothers as a Means of Quality Control," a paper presented by June Solnit Sale at the 51st Annual Meeting of the American Orthopsychiatric Association, San Francisco, April 11, 1974.

needed to improve the quality of life for themselves and those in their care.

By the time the Project had been six months under way, the family day care mothers asked for assistance in planning and establishing an organization to meet their needs. This was the outcome of bringing the total group of 22 Project members together to discuss the issues of a renewal application to OCD. The Project staff took steps to develop a climate in which an organization of family day care mothers could emerge:

- circulation of membership lists, as well as biographies of Project family day care mothers being published in a monthly bulletin.
- a pilot class offered by Pacific Oaks College developed for family day care mothers
- social get-togethers where family day care mothers could begin to know each other in a relaxed and informal setting
- home visits by staff members to talk about the possible implications of forming an organization.

Meanwhile the staff grappled with another concern. We knew from previous experience that the ongoing support and guidance of a trusted organizer was a requirement for the making of an enduring organization. . . .

During the last six months of the Community Family Day Care Project, a staff member was hired for the express purpose of helping the fledgling organization become independent and strong. It must be said here that trying to telescope plans and action into a set timetable was impractical—helping to form and build an organization takes time and patience. (We had the latter, but not the former.)

The first meetings of the organization that were held were staff-controlled in the sense that family day care mothers were assisted by strong directions from staff members. The staff convened the first meetings, suggested agendas, helped to focus on the goals for the organization. Family day care mother leadership emerged, and it was apparent their fine sense of humor and commonsense approach to problem solving would work toward organizational endurance. The original framework which was suggested by the 17 women attending the first meetings was a loosely structured executive committee that provided for revolving responsibility for chairing and conducting meetings and business. After four meetings, the family day care mothers found this unworkable and wanted a more traditional, year-to-year officer-type organization with a constitution, by-laws, dues and an identity.

The staff assisted in making available a number of different constitutions from a variety of other associations and eventually a simple document was composed for the membership to vote upon.... An organizational name was important; the women wanted to be known by a positive, descriptive name. They chose WATCH (Women Attentive to Children's Happiness) from a group of names submitted by members....

Other supports were provided by staff in order to help build WATCH:

- A bulletin that had been produced by the Project was turned over to WATCH; a family day care mother editor was chosen by the members and our staff helped with the technical process.
- The Project toy loan was turned over to WATCH.
- A place to meet was provided by Pacific Oaks College.
- A no-interest loan fund that had been administered by the Project for the purpose of making environmental improvements for family day care homes was turned over to WATCH.
- The beginning of a back-up co-op was formed. This consisted of identifying women who could "back-up" family day care mothers who became ill, went on vacation, or just plain needed a day off.
- The Project had been acting as an information service to large numbers of parents who were in need of child care. WATCH found this service particularly useful to its members and wanted to continue it after the Project closed. This took careful planning. Money was raised so that an ad could be placed; a woman was hired by a WATCH committee; the Project phone listing was changed to WATCH and, by the time of closing, all calls to the Project were switched to the WATCH Information Service.
- A phone tree was initiated so that the women could communicate with each other quickly.

The most important support given by staff was assistance in learning how to work in committees, to work toward achievable goals. Staff members attended all executive and committee meetings to lend what expertise was necessary. As the Project came to a close, less and less help was asked for or needed....

Three of the original group continued their work at Pacific Oaks and were available for continued participation in WATCH on a different and time-limited basis. Our roles changed in some respects and stayed the same in others. We still represented the College and the government to some extent and we found that put us into the role of *experts* and *the enemy* at different times. For example, on a given issue our opinion was asked but our advice was rejected—not on the basis of merit, but rather in a show of independence. This was now the organization of WATCH members and was no longer an extension of the Project; this brought forth both pride and anger.

Staff members were sometimes considered models since it seemed we had more organizational experience than most family day care mothers although, as the organization has progressed, there is little modeling that is necessary. We have served as guides and gatekeepers in understanding the terrain of the community and opening some of the doors that help to strengthen the organization. Most of all, we are now listeners, participants, members and even an officer of WATCH.

WATCH members continue to publish the monthly bulletin. (It has been requested by groups all over the country.) An electric typewriter was purchased, after a fund-raising project, in order to make the cutting of a stencil a bit easier; Pacific Oaks still provides the use of their mimeographing machine. The toy loan has continued, but it is limping along; the problems of breakage and over-use by some members has become a point of concern at meetings. The phone tree operates efficiently, as does the back-up co-op and no-interest loan fund. The information service handles many calls each day and one person has managed the coordination since it began. Problems have arisen, but they are seemingly easily handled by an information service committee. WATCH continues to meet at Pacific Oaks on the second Monday of each month.

Accomplishments of WATCH. WATCH members have participated in several day care conferences. They are vibrant, articulate and marvelous salespersons for family day care. In fact, one family day care mother participated in a panel at [an]. . . . Orthopsychiatric meeting. . . . The president of WATCH has been asked to serve as a vice-president of the Pasadena Child Care Consortium; members have been asked to serve as consultants to a newly formed group of family day care mothers in a nearby community; they have been asked to testify as experts before the City Council when licensing was discussed. In addition, WATCH has signed a letter of intent in order to participate in a Center for Child Development and Educational Therapy proposal to help with early identification of vulnerable children.

WATCH members have been on several local TV and radio shows as well as featured in newspaper stories.

As a group, WATCH members have written two position papers—both in response to direct problems that they have squarely faced. The first paper, *What Is Quality Family Day Care?* was in response to a number of criticisms of family day care that have been carried by the media.

The second position paper was on the subject of discipline. The need for the paper arose from a situation in which a parent claimed that her toddler had been mistreated by a family day care mother, who was a new member of WATCH. After a thorough investigation, it was impossible to determine what the *true* story was: on the one hand there was a distraught pregnant mother who had not told her husband of her need to place their child in some form of care for a few hours a day because she was overtired and very nervous over the impending birth of her second child. On the other side was a family day care mother with little experience in caring for another person's child and who claimed that she had talked to the pregnant mother about the inappropriate way the child was being punished in his own home and being brought to the family day care home in a bruised condition. The problem was raised at a meeting of WATCH and several actions resulted. The new family day care mother was visited but, because of the incident, she stopped caring for children in her home and withdrew her application for a license. A follow-up visit was made to the pregnant mother by staff members in order to see if another home could be found for her child. It was also decided that a paper on discipline should be written that would state WATCH's position and that would be given to each new member of the organization. The first draft of the paper, which was written by a committee of four, was a self-defense document. It described what should be done if a child is brought to a home in a mistreated or bruised condition. In addition, there was a short paragraph on not using cruel and inhumane punishment on children. The information was useful but upon my urging it was decided that a more in-depth exploration of discipline should be written. The final paper was written by a committee and approved by the membership. It takes a commonsense, humanistic and positive attitude of working toward self-discipline, with as little emphasis on punishment as possible.

A packet consisting of both position papers and other informative materials is made available to each member of WATCH. This includes information concerning safety and emergency treatment and tax data as well as the constitution and by-laws and a list of equipment . . . available through the toy loan.

Another spin-off of the discipline crisis was that the back-up co-op was re-emphasized. Family day care mothers agreed that every person who cares for children has a limit in patience and kindness at some time. Should a family day care mother feel that she is reaching that point, she now feels free to call a neighboring member to talk, perhaps visit, or arrange for the care of her children by another member in order to have a few hours of time alone.

Pacific Oaks has continued to offer extension courses that can culminate in a family day care certificate for members of WATCH. Attendance has been less than spectacular since the closing of the Project. . . . This semester we plan to offer a week-end workshop. Family day care mothers tell us that this will fit their time constraints best . . . we will see. In spite of the difficulties, six family day care mothers have received their family day care certificates and three more will complete the requirements next semester.

The content of WATCH meetings varies each month, with an emphasis on business one month and educational and informational discussions the next. The business meetings provide a time for the standing and ad hoc committees to do the work they have established for themselves and to report to the membership on their progress. The educational meetings have diversity with guest speakers such as an attorney speaking about legal responsibilities of day care, an accountant discussing tax problems of day care families, a nutritionist helping to plan good diets for children and adults, a pediatrician exploring child development, and a number of workshops conducted by family day care mothers who have special talents and expertise in such areas as crafts or working with babies or how to present science experience in a home setting.

Problems. One of the perpetual problems that almost any organization faces is that there are *doers, non-doers* and *un-doers*. WATCH is no exception. Our staff members still worry about the building of an elite group, leaving the least articulate out of decisionmaking and perhaps losing those members who most benefit from working together as a group. The membership presently represents widely divergent age grouping, cultural background and socio-economic status. We feel guilty about the little time we spend in helping to encourage the shy and withdrawn women who need a bit of assistance in bringing out ideas that are practical and good. Our good intentions of last year to provide ongoing support to the organization often get lost in here-and-now stresses of our daily jobs.

There has been considerable pressure from without, and at times from within, that all members of WATCH should be licensed family day care mothers. We know that there are few unlicensed members (most have gone through the licensing process since they have joined WATCH), but the importance of keeping the group open to anyone who wants to join (even staff members) is a point of contention that seems to crop up often. There are those who feel that licensing guarantees quality; there are those who know it does not. Staff members know most of the members; programs and, often, standards and quality are in the mind of the beholder. Time and again, the point is made that the purpose of WATCH is to provide quality care for children by including rather than excluding all of those interested in achieving this end. We are not sure what will happen to this issue, but it does raise another important point for consideration.

Another problem has arisen from the fact that some family day care mothers have joined WATCH with the idea that they will receive an unlimited number of referrals from the information service. When this doesn't happen, they are angry.... Some members of WATCH want to return their membership dues and read them out of the organization; the majority are attempting to interest them in attending at least one meeting in the hope that they will become interested and participate in the growth of WATCH.

One reason why the June Solnit Sale paper is having and will continue to have a major influence on the development of Associations is that it describes the formation, organization and maintenance of an Association in detail, without implying that theirs is the only way Associations *should* develop and function. This approach will encourage those who want a "how to do it" model that leaves them free to adapt for their own situations.

An official of a publicly supported state agency for children reports:

We are beginning to organize independent family day care providers in a geographical area where there are a sufficient number of licensed providers to begin to encourage people to come together. It is an entirely voluntary kind of thing. We find that it works well if there is one fairly sophisticated family day care provider in the area who can lend enthusiasm to the issues. So far there has been a very good response. It looks as though there is a lot of potential in doing this kind of organization. It doesn't involve any money, most of what the focus is on are the kinds of problems day care providers experience in the operation dealing with parents. They are beginning to do their own seeking of answers but some are asking that we help them.

They've also decided that they would like to set up a very informal kind of referral system first off, since one or two well-established providers have people calling them all the time. They're well known in the community and if they are full, then there are always people waiting. They've been successful in doing that kind of referral among themselves. They want some kind of informal mechanism for loaning each other things like cribs. The attitude with which we are approaching these independent networks is that we're looking for them to be interested—we're not working to organize them except to act as a catalyst and be a resource if we can help solve problems. Beyond that it will be their own interest that sustains them.

A brief description of the way another Association operates was provided by the director of an organization acting as an advocate for women and children:

We were asked by the Association of Welfare home day care providers in a neighboring state to help them take their case to the public, especially the legislature. They are not saying, "Pay us what we deserve," because they know no woman is being paid what she deserves, whether you are a housewife at home with your own kids or you're working in a day care center or are a schoolteacher. They are saying, "Times are hard, the twelve dollars a week doesn't even cover costs." They think what they are doing is vital and important and they want to make that plain. They're asking us to help them find a model for the kind of Association and professional consultant they want.

It seems likely that Associations will continue to grow and be an important element in bringing together both formal and informal family day care givers in networks of Associations having an important influence on family day care. The next few years will inevitably also see the kind of strife that characterizes the formation and maintenance of organizations devoted to improving their members' professional lives. Who should be admitted and under what conditions and, conversely, who should be excluded are concerns to educational, medical, and law associations and to many others. The problems in family day care are compounded by the fact that there are no universally accepted standards of admission, such as education, and the strength of these organizations may well lie in their *inclusiveness* rather then the customary organizational drive toward *exclusion*.

A question rarely asked but of considerable importance is whether family day care users should be included in Associations. At the present time we know of no instances where this pertains nor even if an effort has been made to include them. It can be argued that no organization with an occupational base includes users of the service—the American Medical Association does not have patients as members, nor the Bar Association, litigants. But we suggest that family day care is a different kind of occupation and that ultimately the welfare of the children is dependent on the mutual satisfaction of givers and users. The issues affecting the givers also affect users, and there is a great deal of role reversal that one doesn't see in other occupations. It would be interesting to observe the progess of an Association including both givers and users. The history of other organizations suggests that the next few years will be stormy ones for Associations; that their chances for a successful, useful future rest on the kind of working partnership that preserves the spontaneity, talent, and self-direction of the family day care giver from every background and involves the organizational expertise and community understanding of professionals.

CHAPTER 6

THE DAY CARE NEIGHBOR SERVICE

There is another new kind of family day care service which appears to have promise for increasing the quality and quantity of family day care at every socio-economic level—certainly a comprehensive claim but one founded on experience seasoned with pride, for the authors of this book spent ten years developing the service we have regularly referred to from the beginning of the book and come to call Day Care Neighbor Service. It is, like most other useful approaches to day care needs, really an institutionalization of a natural custom, adaptable for use in formal and informal day care programs. In fact, there is much overlap in the functions of the information and referral services, Associations, and Day Care Neighbor Services that suggests they can support each other in many ways.

We described the Day Care Neighbor Service in a Handbook* whose purpose was to encourage replication and further experimentation with this new form of partnership between professionals and non-professionals. Since the handbook, though out of print for some time, is still being requested, most of it is reprinted here, with some exclusions and with additions gained from later experience.

What the Day Care Neighbor Service Is

The Day Care Neighbor Service is a way of improving the quality and quantity of day care for children cared for in the homes of nonrelatives. It makes use of a social-work consultant to find the

*The Day Care Neighbor Service: A Handbook for the Organization and Operation of a New Approach to Family Day Care by Alice H. Collins and Eunice L. Watson (Portland, Ore.: Tri-County Community Council, 1969).

key individual in each neighborhood already informally helping her neighbors make day care arrangements. These may be women who want day care for their children or who want children to care for. Though their experience as both users and givers often has provided them with good understanding of both roles, they have usually chosen to be home-based when they are identified and acting in the Day Care Neighbor role. The social-work consultant assists these key individuals—called *Day Care Neighbors*—to become active: in recruiting more and better day care givers; in matching givers and users who will be compatible and helpful to the children; and in maintaining good arrangements which might otherwise terminate. The social-work consultant confines her* contacts to twelve to fifteen Day Care Neighbors, who in turn have contacts with fifty to seventy-five families a year with whom consultants have no direct contact. The central focus of the service is helping home-centered individuals already performing a neighborhood service continue their chosen natural role with a higher degree of success.

The Day Care Neighbor Service is built around people like Mrs. Smith:

Mrs. Smith's children are in their early teens. She is no longer busy all the time keeping house and looking after them, but she feels she should be at home when they are and besides she likes her home and has no special job skills or career goals. Her husband prefers her to be home, too. She does have an interest in helping others and is especially interested in children. She has always been a kind of babysitting resource for her friends. Mrs. Smith is likely to "watch the children" when a neighbor has a beauty or medical appointment or wants to do a few hours shopping. There are always extra children in and out of the house. Neighbors drop in on Mrs. Smith, too, for a cup of coffee or a chat about the good and bad things going on at home; to use the washing machine when theirs has broken down; or to get a new recipe or describe a successful one.

Once or twice, when a neighbor has gone on a trip or there has been serious and prolonged illness in a neighbor's family, Mrs. Smith has made a regular arrangement to look after a young child every day and been paid for

*The consultant is referred to in the feminine throughout the account of the Day Care Neighbor Service because we found that male consultants, though no less skillful, were less acceptable as frequent, informal callers to both the Day Care Neighbors and their husbands. Until more enlightened times change this kind of prejudice, we believe it best for the social-work consultants to Day Care Neighbors to be women.

it. Now, when the increased costs of teenage needs has put some strain on the family budget, she wonders if she could pick up some extra money by daily babysitting for one or two children. This would bring in a little income, let her remain at home, avoid the expenses attached to going out to work, and do some good for children, whom she enjoys for themselves.

Learning and meeting license requirements is no problem for Mrs. Smith nor for the people who want her to look after their children, and soon she is "babysitting" a two-year-old of a friend who has returned to nursing, and the four-year-old of another, who, having just been divorced, is taking a secretarial course. News that Mrs. Smith now is an "official" babysitter moves with amazing rapidity over the neighborhood grapevine. The nurse tells the dietician at the hospital, whose sister-in-law is looking for someone to take care of her baby. A neighbor mentions it to a friend dissatisfied with her present arrangement. Mrs. Smith begins to get requests for care of children of strangers as well as those of friends.

She wants to go on as she always has, taking the children along when she goes to the store or does other errands, keeping them in the house or outdoors as the weather allows. In short, she does not want to change her lifestyle, but it makes her feel a little out of it and maybe selfish to just do what she likes at home while she knows about the need for good child care and her ability and pleasure in giving it. There are examples in abundance in the neighborhood:

Cherie Jones is on AFDC and wants desperately to take training as a beautician so she can become financially independent. She is only nineteen and has two very little children. Her husband deserted her. Obviously, the children need home life experience and, from the way Cherie talks, she could use a sympathetic older woman to talk to and get some advice from, too.

Then there are the Brown boys in first and second grade. School opens two hours after their parents must leave for work. It is amazing how much trouble they get into in the neighborhood because they are at loose ends and really too young to be left alone. And only last week, at the PTA meeting, the principal stated that there are entirely too many children appearing at school as early as seven or seven-thirty. The school can provide no supervision and the children are getting into difficulties that may become quite serious.

Since she began babysitting, a number of Mrs. Smith's friends and acquaintances have remarked, "I wouldn't mind taking on a couple of kids myself if I knew how to find them." So, when Mrs. Smith begins to think about how to help someone when she cannot, she may suggest a person she knows is interested in doing babysitting.

She tends to think of someone giving the same quality of care she does, since she is apt to think of the needs of children rather than the simple expedience a harried mother might resort to when temporarily desperate for someone to care for her children so she can accept an urgent job offer.

Mrs. Smith may even look for someone who hasn't mentioned babysitting or ever done it before—Mrs. Grant, for example, down the street, not too young, but still brisk and energetic though lonely since her husband died and her family lives in another state. Like many elderly people she gets up very early and has her small amount of housework all finished and a long empty day ahead of her by breakfast time. What about getting her to give the Brown boys breakfast and a send-off to school, since their mother has to be at work in the plant cafeteria by seven o'clock—and a snack after school just before she picks them up? Without realizing it, or doing it in any formal sense, Mrs. Smith becomes a kind of day care exchange in the neighborhood as well as widening the circle of people to whom she gives advice and emotional support and the benefit of her interest and experience with children.

In the initial phase of our project* to demonstrate a new kind of family day care service, studies and observation of people like Mrs. Smith convinced us that they live in almost all neighborhoods where there are young families with children. In our first close looks at people like Mrs. Smith we noted they were very skillful at matching givers and users, finding and persuading new people to give needed day care, and providing the listening ear and peacemaking word that might keep an arrangement going that would otherwise break up. At other times, it was apparent that there were difficulties needing professional attention. These usually involved very young children and seemed to offer unique opportunities for preventing later difficulties.

The studies that opened our eyes to the way certain people function as informal exchange agents in neighborhoods also alerted us to the tremendous number of such arrangements initiated, broken, and remade almost daily. We recognized, somewhat painfully, that from our customary position as social workers in a central agency it was extremely difficult to judge the quality of care a child would receive. We could see that neighbors without professional training were indeed in a better position to make such judgments.

It seemed to us that if we could find and recruit people like Mrs.

---

*The Day Care Exchange Project, Children's Bureau, D-135.

Smith, we could join them, contributing our professional skills to their natural neighborly ones, and supporting their ability to recruit, match, and maintain day care arrangements. Together, we might make a useful team, improving the day care for many children whom neither of us alone might be able to help. The Day Care Neighbor Service grew out of our conviction that this notion was an exciting one to test out in action.

Planning a Day Care Neighbor Service

The how-to approach we use in the following pages may seem to imply that this is the *only* way in which a family day care service should be done. Nothing could be further from the truth. We believe there should be many kinds of day care services, and we hope the Day Care Neighbor Service, either as we describe it or in any of its many variations, may be one among many useful services. It is true, too, that rather than qualify all our statements, we sometimes sound as though our advice is the result of long experimentation. It is not, but rather derives from three distinct Day Care Neighbor Services in neighborhoods of the widest possible socioeconomic differences: one is in the northwest section of a well-established city; another in its more recently settled southeast, and the other in two trailer courts in an adjoining county. Since our own project terminated, we have looked at a number of others using similar concepts but with different kinds of network populations—the aged, for one, and minorities having emotional and health problems, and we have been glad to see that others have also discovered the usefulness of natural networks. We hope the years ahead will see many more such experiments and accounts of them that will help us all enlarge, modify, and adjust our concepts and techniques.

Who Should Undertake a Day Care Neighbor Service?

We believe the Day Care Neighbor Service may be incorporated into the ongoing operation of day care centers, public and private, family and child care agencies, community mental health services, PTA's, industries or businesses employing many women, schools, and community action programs. This service is not primarily intended to be a new and autonomous agency, but rather part of the total services of existing facilities. There is no reason, however, why it could not be a self-sustaining agency if for some reason this seemed most desirable.

Assessing Need

A survey to determine whether day care is needed and in what amount seems to be a usual first step before establishing a service. As noted above, these surveys are not always reliable predictions of future use though they are always time-consuming, difficult to construct and execute, and expensive. In addition, in the field of day care they often raise unrealistic hopes that may prove damaging to a service which, when established, cannot meet advance expectations.

There are a number of other ways of determining a suitable locale for a Day Care Neighbor Service. School as well as national statistics, the informal opinions of school and health personnel, employers, and the many other private citizens might be consulted. Existing statistics may not be up to date, however, and cannot predict unforeseen changes affecting use, such as labor-market changes, population shifts, the growth of new neighborhoods and deterioration of old ones.

Whatever method is chosen for determining need, consideration must be given to other existing day care facilities in the area—their cost, availability, and acceptance by the community. Obviously, a Day Care Neighbor Service will be most needed and most likely to succeed in neighborhoods where there is a preponderance of young families with children, many working mothers, and some not working.

AREA AND POPULATION TO BE SERVED

The Day Care Neighbor Service is based on the assumption that there are persons like Mrs. Smith who have a central place in their neighborhood system and can be recruited as Day Care Neighbors. It follows therefore that a Day Care Neighbor Service will function best if prospective users and givers live within definable, rather small neighborhoods. But it is not possible to be definitive about what comprises a "neighborhood." Some neighborhoods consist of single houses covering a relatively large area; others of one or several high-rise apartment houses in only part of a city block. Those who live in the neighborhood and professionals who work there usually know the visible and invisible boundaries defining them and can describe them in practical if not theoretical terms. Therefore an agency may well begin by reviewing home addresses of those it seeks to serve and plotting them on a map, giving consideration to geographic and social boundaries. Organizations already serving defined neighborhoods can, of course, safely skip this first step.

The prospective sponsoring agency will also need to determine the size of the service. To date, experience has shown that one Day Care Neighbor can be in touch with fifty to seventy-five families in a year and one social-work consultant can maintain contact with twelve to fifteen Day Care Neighbors at a time. An agency seeking to serve a relatively small number of its clients might free a staff member's time sufficiently to have her act as consultant to one or two Day Care Neighbors in small neighborhoods. Another facility with a large clientele, or an agency solely devoted to providing day care (such as a Day Care Center) might plan for one staff member whose sole responsibility would be consultation with twelve to fifteen Day Care Neighbors, each residing in a separate neighborhood.

ARE EXPECTATIONS REALISTIC

The urgency of need and tendency to confuse the service with a kind of businesslike employment agency may lead to expectations that will prove unrealistic. The Day Care Neighbor Service will *not* meet all the community's day care needs shortly after it is organized or at any time in the future. It is more realistic to see the service's goal as the relatively modest improvement of present family day care. Considering the very large numbers involved in day care, this is no small objective.

How Should a Day Care Neighbor Service Be Staffed?

A Day Care Neighbor Service depends on a partnership between the consultant and the Day Care Neighbors whose work is facilitated by the clerical staff.

THE SOCIAL WORK CONSULTANT

At present, we feel that the Day Care Neighbor Service consultant should be a social worker with full professional training and the experience to be able to use consultation method. The consultant will need the flexibility to accept the Day Care Neighbor as a partner, just as she would do with a teacher, nurse, or other more usual consultee, recognizing that each has equally important—though different—responsibilities. She will also need to be able to maintain regular communication with staff from her own organization and others for mutual support, the exchange of significant impressions, and future planning.

THE DAY CARE NEIGHBOR

The first task of the consultant is to find and recruit Day Care Neighbors. Education, age, and previous work experience are not reliable guides to selecting Day Care Neighbors. Their status is unique in that they are neither employees of an agency with a set of standards to be met as a condition of employment nor volunteers in the sense of donating a given amount of time to perform unpaid tasks assigned to them by an agency staff member. They cannot be selected according to their leadership standing in the community because Day Care Neighbors are usually home-centered women who cooperate with leaders but do not act in that capacity. How then are they to be described? In formulating a list of the characteristics we looked for, we learned that we sought women who were:

- actively involved in the neighborhood day care system, caring regularly for the children of others and recognized as day care resource persons by their friends and neighbors;
- part of an intact family with children in the home;
- home-centered in their interests and lifestyle;

- helpful to their neighbors in many ways that were so natural to them and accepted by others that they were hardly aware of what they did;
- sufficiently concerned and with enough energy to become involved with others outside their immediate families without depriving their own families;
- likely to be involved with a number of projects concerned with children, such as Scouts, Campfire, church groups, 4-H, PTA, family foster care, and so on. Most successful Day Care Neighbors proved to be very busy people, but able to manage these activities easily and efficiently;
- relatively free of "drain" in their personal lives. Emotional drain may have little relationship to actual life circumstances; persons on welfare may be free of it while those at considerably higher incomes may feel unequal to the demands made on them by their daily lives, or vice versa.

CLERICAL EMPLOYEES

The clerical work of most Day Care Services is not complicated. It involves answering telephone calls and keeping records. It is important to have staff who have a pleasant telephone manner, who are interested and concerned but not intrusive since they will transfer calls whenever possible to Day Care Neighbors. Accuracy and determination are needed to maintain records which may be received in informal ways—in rough notes or on tape—rather than on standard forms. It is vitally important to the future of the service that accurate use statistics and other information be available. We found that Day Care Neighbors themselves were often encouraged to note from the statistics that they really *had* "been doing something." If computerization is possible, of course the clerical staff will need to understand how to cooperate in this program.

What Will the Service Cost?

Cost depends so largely on the size of the service and its auspices that it can be discussed only in quite general terms.

The consultant should be paid at the prevailing rate for a senior caseworker. We consider that one consultant can be expected to work with twelve to fifteen Day Care Neighbors. A small service might use a part-time consultant or purchase part-time service from an existing agency such as a mental health center.

An already functioning agency might want to make use of a Day Care Neighbor component to serve a designated clientele and might free a member of its staff to act as a consultant. What the salary of the consultant should be would need to be decided in terms of time, based on the full-time scale.

Since it is agreed that the Day Care Neighbors have an unprecedented position, it is difficult to know how, or even if, they should be paid. We settled on a token stipend of twenty-five dollars a month and offered it as a mark of our appreciation of their willingness to talk with us and to keep some records. We made it clear that there would be no way of measuring what their financial *value* might be, nor could we possibly pay them the very large sums that would be commensurate with it. The Day Care Neighbors from all economic levels expressed their satisfaction with the token payment. When, in one instance, payment had to be discontinued for lack of funds, they universally expressed their willingness to continue to serve, stating in various ways that the pay was nice because it made them feel they were really "part of something," but they said that they had always carried on without pay before they knew us and would continue to do so now.

There is some possibility for Day Care Neighbors to earn a steadier income from their caregiving when they are part of an organized Day Care Neighbor Service because they are free to take on the children referred to them, sometimes assuring a less fluctuating income. We made it plain, however, that there was no expectation that they must take on anyone so that they were free to use this source of additional income or not, at their own discretion.

Clerical staff should be paid at the prevailing rate, with some value being placed on their personal qualities as well as clerical skills. We believe a half-time clerical worker can provide the necessary services for a full-time consultant.

Funds for consultant transportation must also be included in the budget. They will obviously vary in accordance to the geographic area to be covered.

Customary overhead expenses for housing, utilities, telephone, and employee coverage must, of course, be budgeted. Since interviewing is always done at the Day Care Neighbor's home, office space is not needed for it. In general, space requirements are not large. Probably the most economical arrangement would be to have the Day Care Neighbor Service connected with an information and referral service or a day care center.

Finding the Day Care Neighbors

The first task of the consultant is to find her future partners—the Day Care Neighbors. The obvious place to begin the search is in the neighborhood that has been selected as in need of the service. In some instances the social-work consultant may already have an intimate knowledge of the neighborhood and its residents. Assuming this is not the case, she will want to get the feel of the neighborhood by walking or riding about the streets, noting where and how children play, observing family patterns, neighborhood stores, and street activity. Day care patterns may sometimes be understood from observation of morning and evening traffic of parents with young children.

Since Day Care Neighbors are recruited from the ranks of those already giving day care, the consultant will want to ask questions about day care givers wherever possible. It is best to ask "Is there babysitting around here?" and "Do people seem to have a hard time finding it?" rather than ask directly for names of givers. Local cafes, drugstores, small groceries; school secretaries, ministers, and public health nurses; advertisements in local papers, on laundromat bulletin boards, and places of employment are all good sources of general information, and easily accessible.

Our experience suggests that the initial response in most middle-class neighborhoods is "There are no working mothers around here and no one does babysitting." In poor neighborhoods, the consultant is at first likely to be seen as trying to "get something on" day care givers and users and information is withheld. A few more interested and objective inquiries, such as "If you or your neighbor needed a babysitter, who would you ask to help you find one?" may elicit some names of others to be contacted.

The consultant should keep preliminary contacts quite casual in order to avoid establishing herself as the central figure in the projected Day Care Neighbor Service and to minimize agency involvement to give the service a neighborhood, not an agency, "image."

Through the widening circle of brief contacts made by following up suggestions by visits or telephone, the consultant will probably get names of possible Day Care Neighbors, and a good deal of incidental neighborhood information about each one. For example, a day care giver described as having "a house full of babies all the time," or one who is obliging about babysitting at any time for any number of children would be a doubtful candidate. She may not be sensitive to the individual needs of children. There is more than a possibility that her day care activity is an effort to stem severe emotional or financial drain. On the other hand, someone described as "not really doing babysitting" but a friend who takes care of the informant's children "just now" or as a person "who knows everything about the neighborhood" would be a likely prospect.

MAKING DAY CARE NEIGHBOR CONTACTS

When several likely prospects have been mentioned several times in this admittedly long, drawn-out process, the consultant may telephone each possible candidate, explain that she has been mentioned as knowledgeable about day care which is of interest to the caller, too. It should be made clear at once that the caller is not looking for a babysitter, but simply wants to chat with someone who knows a lot about how it is given in the neighborhood. If the person is responsive—and most people like to share their expertise—an appointment can be made with special stress on its being at a time convenient for the neighborhood day care expert.

This first contact with the prospective Day Care Neighbor may be the beginning of a long-term relationship and so has considerable significance. It is likely that the interview will not cause much concern to the prospective Day Care Neighbor. She will be used to having people come to see her and ask her advice about community or personal problems. She is likely to receive the consultant as she would a minister, school principal, or a neighbor—with friendliness and hospitality, on the assumption that she will help if she can; she will have no anxiety concerning her competence to do so.

The consultant, on the other hand, may find this interview somewhat difficult. The consultant will have initiated the contact and asked for help and advice, both actions which differ from the usual ways a professional enters contacts.

Unlike more conventional intake interviews, the social worker will not have a well-defined set of questions in mind. Rather, she will attempt to gain a general impression both of the neighborhood day care system and the potential Day Care Neighbor as a person in her own community. There is no prescribed length for such an interview. The consultant must be sensitive to the Day Care Neighbor's style and recognize whether or not she should settle in for a long diffuse chat.

Whether the interview is long or short, anticipate a good many interruptions. In fact, these interruptions help an alert consultant make some decisions about the suitability of the potential Day Care Neighbor. If there are people dropping in for coffee on the way to an appointment, leaving off a child to "watch" till their return, the phone ringing with an urgent invitation to take on some committee job or deal with a family crisis, it is likely that this is indeed the home of someone seen as a central figure in the neighborhood.

The consultant will not have quite such obvious clues as to "freedom from drain," but they, too, will be seen in the prospective Day Care Neighbor's manner, which ideally is responsive, concerned, active, and relaxed at the same time.

A potential Day Care Neighbor may seem rather reticent about responding to direct questions about neighborhood day care arrangements which she may view as gossip. She will be more likely to comment on the children playing in and around the house; to answer the consultant's questions about them with pleasure and interest, showing remarkably complete knowledge of their family background, ability to get along with their peers, and general school adjustment. She will be perceptive and positive rather than critical or destructive in talking about others.

If the day care giver impresses the consultant as a good prospect, this will be the time to describe the Day Care Neighbor Service in general terms, noting reactions. Our experience was that good prospects grasped the idea quickly, identified themselves as "acting like Day Care Neighbors," and gave other indications of interest. The consultant may end the interview by asking if she may return for another chat. We found we made the best decisions if we postponed actual recruitment until we had seen all prospects. No candidate is perfect, however, and delaying a decision too long may reflect a consultant's or an agency's anxiety about this unaccustomed way of working with people rather than any personal deficiency of the prospective Day Care Neighbor.

Recruitment

When a decision has been reached, the consultant may telephone the prospect and ask for another appointment. The people we approached had little hesitation and agreed readily. This did not necessarily imply their full understanding of what we were asking of them. Such an understanding only comes about slowly. Nevertheless, at the recruitment interview the consultant should take the time to:

- sketch why the day care giver selected seems well suited to the role of Day Care Neighbor, emphasizing her knowledge of the neighborhood, friendliness, and obvious interest in others;
- describe the Day Care Neighbor Service in detail, even if this has been done previously, with special emphasis on the freedom the Day Care Neighbor will have to continue to function as she has done in the past, to take on or refuse care of additional day care children;
- mention record-keeping and the acceptance of requests from givers and users not now known to the Day Care Neighbor;
- explain token payment made for her service;
- describe the consultant-Day Care Neighbor relationship as a partnership, and offer a period of weekly appointments to be spaced to monthly intervals as acquaintance increases;
- suggest that she be readily available by telephone.

FROM A SOCIAL WORK CONSULTANT'S RECRUITMENT RECORD

6/5——Contacted the school secretary, B. School. She said the director of the B. Park Community Center is to be away for the summer but would be a good resource for information. The Catholic Church Sodality Group, like the ladies' aid societies in other churches, might be a resource for learning about day care here. Two foster mothers in the area might be helpful. Mrs. B. is "a doll" with many women leaning on her for advice. Mrs. R.D., black past president of the PTA, and Mrs. D. are people who know everyone." ... The public health nurse, Mrs. L., was ill much of the year so won't have current information. Mrs. D.S. does a lot of babysitting, but "I wouldn't leave my cat there." The juvenile-court counselor might know families in the area. The woolen mill at the south end of the neighborhood hires a number of mothers whose children are in school at B., but the mothers don't tell the personnel office about their babysitting problems!

7/11——Telephoned both Mrs. R.D. and Mrs. D. (connected with the PTA). They both named Mrs. E. and Mrs. C.C. as people others would turn to for advice and child care. Mrs. D. thought that many children came to school early before school opens because they didn't have care at home. Mrs. D. used to give day care herself, but has discontinued due to her many volunteer activities. Mrs. C.C., according to Mrs. D., not only gives day care but also takes children in foster care. She is the one neighbors turn to in cases of emergency. Mrs. D. said the local paper runs ads for child care, and suggested this as a resource. She thinks there is some exchanging of day care giving in the neighborhood. The close neighbors she has, eight to ten houses around, mostly have older kids out of school or in college. She has little contact with parents of preschool children and has less neighborliness than when she had preschool children.

7/17——Met with Rev. F. at his home by appointment. He was looking after his own children while his wife was working. He mentioned:

Mrs. B.: This is a second marriage for two teachers, one had six and the other had four children, and they have used day care in the past. He didn't know whether they were currently using day care.

Mrs. T.: Is known as a helping neighbor. She gives board and room for a child from the Deaf School and has given day care to a granddaughter.

Mrs. E.: Gives temporary day care for a retarded child.

Mrs. H.: Both parents work and there are three young children so he thinks they use child care.

He commented that there were a lot of apartments going up in the area and that many of these permitted children, although some were geared to single people.

Mrs. Z.: Recommended her very highly. Lives next door to the church and takes care of only one child at a time. She refers requests for care to a friend, a Mrs. S., when she is full. She's on Social Security, and day care is her only source of earned income.

D.S.: Is a young woman, nineteen or twenty. She is a school dropout and had a forced marriage. Her one boy is a preschooler, and she is making every effort to succeed as a mother and wife. She might be a potential resource as a giver.

B. district covered six elementary school districts selected for heterogeneous representation of the city at large. In all, ninety-two contacts were made in B. district before six women were asked to become Day Care Neighbors. All accepted.

In acting as consultants with Day Care Neighbors we had to recognize our own initial anxiety and refrain from projecting it onto the Day Care Neighbors. The Day Care Neighbors were all women with healthy self-concepts, well aware of neighborhood needs and their ability to help meet them. When we accepted their reluctance and doubts and assured them of our willingness to wait until they had thought the whole matter over and discussed it further with their husbands and reassured them about the records, they regained interest and enthusiasm. No Day Care Neighbor voluntarily withdrew after an initial commitment.

FIRST INTERVIEWS

To a consultant accustomed to interviewing in an office arranged for privacy, home interviewing with a Day Care Neighbor as an ongoing plan may at first seem too time-consuming and distracting. The caseworker from a public agency may have some difficulty shifting from a worker-client relationship to a partnership. Home interviews should be carried on throughout the life of the service, however, because they:

- act out for the Day Care Neighbor the friendly colleague relationship as opposed to a more formal specialist-to-layman or caseworker-to-client approach;
- demonstrate the consultant's willingness to accommodate to the demands of the busy active life of successful Day Care Neighbors;

- help the consultant understand the Day Care Neighbor's neighborhood with its own customs, values, and way of functioning, related to many variations in family income, geography, ethnic origin, and so on.

With these objectives in mind, then, the consultant will begin her contacts with the Day Care Neighbor in accordance with the Day Care Neighbor's own style. The consultant will focus on activity rather than on feelings or attitudes; on the specifics of day care arrangements rather than general theories of child care and development. The consultant and the Day Care Neighbor will both be reassured by discussing practical details of their partnership.

Several major topics are likely to be foremost:

- How will those needing service know of the Day Care Neighbor's interest and willingness to provide it?
- How will the consultant know what is going on when face-to-face contact with the Day Care Neighbor will be brief and occur at widely spaced intervals?
- How can the consultant learn enough about the neighborhood to offer the Day Care Neighbor support and assistance in increasing her scope?

Operating the Service: Starting Up

Making the Service More Widely Known

Day Care Neighbors should be encouraged to use any method that seems natural and attractive to let others know of their willingness to help in making day care arrangements and advising about them. The consultant may wish to suggest a number of ways that have been successful for others, but should avoid being too direct since the Day Care Neighbor will have her own style with which she is most comfortable.

In our project Day Care Neighbors:

- told their friends informally about their new role, letting word of mouth convey it to other neighbors they did not know;

- discussed the Day Care Neighbor Service and their part in it at church group meetings, PTA's, women's clubs, nursery schools, or other semiformal gatherings where there were working mothers and home-staying mothers;
- informed school and church secretaries of their activities and their willingness to try to make child care matches;
- placed advertisements in neighborhood newspapers, PTA bulletins, industrial or business house organs, or other relatively accessible media of communication.

How the Day Care Neighbor Can Keep Track of Neighborhood Activity

Record-keeping may seem unsuitable for discussion in early interviews, since it is not a natural part of the Day Care Neighbor's role. On the other hand, record-keeping emphasizes the importance of knowing about neighborhood activity and helps the Day Care Neighbor supply significant data to the central service. Day Care Neighbors will expect to keep some records and will expect to be instructed about them. They may also be quite apprehensive about their ability to keep records. For these reasons it has already been suggested that the consultant talk about records right from the beginning of the contact.

A decision about what records should be kept and their design should precede the consultant's visits to the Day Care Neighbors. The consultant should then take along examples of forms and explain carefully how they are to be used. Explain, too, how the collected statistics will be used in the central office. Emphasize the contribution records will make to the value of the whole agency as they increase understanding of need and use customs.

Even the most careful explanation, however, will not entirely allay the concern the Day Care Neighbor may feel about writing things down about her neighbors, which sometimes seems like a kind of gossip. But we found Day Care Neighbors responded to our point that gossip could be benign or malignant—that interest in the affairs of one's neighbors in order to assist them seemed to us a benign form of gossip and entirely legitimate. We assured Day Care Neighbors that we would respect their confidences although we avoided equating this with the confidentiality accorded to private communications in a caseworker-client context, to avoid the clinical analogy.

Consultants should bear in mind that while Day Care Neighbors may tend to be careless about record-keeping, consultants tend to overvalue accuracy, which may predispose them to placing Day Care Neighbors in the position of guilty children who have not done their homework rather than knowledgeable and very busy colleagues.

Sometimes information related to requests for service requires a longer explanation than a Day Care Neighbor wants to write on the record card. If a tape recorder is available and the consultant feels comfortable in using it, she may offer to bring it to the monthly record-collecting interview. The Day Care Neighbor can then be encouraged to keep only a skeleton record of contacts to remind her of things she wants to talk about with the consultant with the tape recorder running. Later, pertinent facts and comments can be transferred to the appropriate cards in the office.

Tapes of this kind, and also complete recorded interviews between consultant and Day Care Neighbors, proved invaluable to us in perfecting our interviewing skills and in noting all kinds of small, significant comments we would have missed because of our active involvement in the interviewing process. But it is imperative to have a plan for transcribing recordings without delays; few projects can afford to double interview time, which happens if the later analysis of the interview is re-heard rather than read.

We anticipated a good deal of difficulty in accustoming Day Care Neighbors (and perhaps ourselves) to using a tape recorder, but it proved to be no problem at all.

DCN: Different ones come to see me about different projects; now, just like getting a church club started up here last year—through the school. So I don't know—whether it's because I've lived here so long in this neighborhood or what.

SWC: Would you be willing, do you think, to put this down on a record card and then I could——

DCN: Lord, I wouldn't know how to put it down on paper.

SWC: If I could help you with it, would you be willing to try it? We could use the tape recorder so we wouldn't have to write so much down while we're talking.

DCN: Well, I could try...

SWC: This isn't for you to do anything differently than what you are, as far as the other people are concerned. It would be just talking about contacts you had with Mrs. J. and the children—whatever you wanted to tell me.

DCN: I could put down my neighbor—Mrs. L.S. takes care of two little ones, one that is eleven and one eight years old, coming there on weekends to stay so many hours while the mother is working.... I think she got them from up there at the store...

SWC: How does she like it?

DCN: She likes it fine, because she likes children too, like I do, and so she's lonesome staying there at the house with her husband at school and that's why she wants to get her some more to babysit with. She's got two more that she keeps—let's see—Monday... Tuesday, Wednesday, I guess. Then the rest of the week, the mother's home with 'em.

SWC: How did she find those?

DCN: Well, there's a lady that lives up the street here—she used to work with her at the diner up there and when she quit working, she got L. to sort of take care of her little ones then while she was sleeping. She worked at night and she likes to sleep a few hours during the daytime so L. watches the kids while she is resting.

SWC: Well, as you come in contact with people, maybe you'll keep track of this for us, which might make you hear of more if, you know, if you're thinking about it.

DCN: Well, you know, really, I haven't paid any attention to how many, you know, babysitters there are in this neighborhood...

SWC: We thought maybe if you had a record card like this, you know, that you could just jot down every time someone talked to you about this. Then I could come by and we could get more of the details. I certainly have learned a lot already.

How the Consultant Can Learn More About the Neighborhood

One device that will help Day Care Neighbors describe neighborhood arrangements more fully is to make a map of the neighborhood. A rough sketch with graphic placement of persons discussed serves several purposes at this stage of the Day Care Neighbor-consultant relationship:

- The Day Care Neighbor is likely to consult her husband and children in making the map, thus involving them in her Day Care Neighbor undertaking.

- Making a map may bring to mind people who may have potential for giving or wanting day care who might be overlooked.
- In future contacts at wider intervals it gives the consultant a basis for making inquiries about people who might not have been recalled and reported.

The map, like other "getting started" devices, is only as useful as it seems attractive to the Day Care Neighbor. If she does not respond to the consultant's suggestion, it should not be pursued.

Beginning a Partnership

While practical subjects provide the major agenda for first interviews, the beginning of the relationship between Day Care Neighbor and consultant is of no less importance. In discussing practical subjects the Day Care Neighbor will probably talk about her own children and husband, and sometimes about her own childhood, especially as it relates to babysitting. Naturally the consultant will be interested in hearing what the Day Care Neighbor tells her spontaneously but the consultant should remember that this conversation is not a clinical interview and it's likely that the Day Care Neighbor's views and theories of child-raising are as valid as her own. This does not mean that the consultant need agree with everything the Day Care Neighbor tells her or need respond with a discussion of her own family and views, but rather that she must assume the position of any new acquaintance, perhaps with additional emphasis on her general interest in children.

The consultant will do well to remember that the Day Care Neighbor is a natural expert in human relations and that she, too, is making observations, consciously or unconsciously, in this interview. The Day Care Neighbor will expect the consultant to accept her as a competent, independent person.

The relationship the consultant strives to create between herself and the Day Care Neighbor is unique; its goal: to provide each other with sufficient information to establish a friendly partnership in which both are free to offer opinions, ask questions, differ or agree on ways of helping neighborhood families make day care arrangements that will be satisfactory. This goal does not involve effecting major change in personality or functioning of the Day Care Neighbor. The consultant does have the responsibility, rather, of using professional techniques for diagnosing difficulties a Day Care Neighbor may have carrying out her role, and thus decrease these difficulties and increase satisfying functioning.

Helping Day Care Neighbors Take an Official Role

TIMING ORGANIZATION OF THE SERVICE

Initially, Day Care Neighbors are likely to fear being swamped with calls or having more to do than they can manage, given their home responsibilities. This may also be a silent concern of the consultant. There is probably some possibility that this will occur in some areas, since there always seems to be some imbalance between the numbers of people wanting to give care and those wanting to use it. But we found that demand built slowly, that consultants and Day Care Neighbors both were more anxious when there were only a few requests than when there were many. One way of diminishing anxiety is to begin the service at a time of known high demand. Employment services can tell when this can be expected. In our community, for example, we found peak periods when older children returned to school in the fall, and after Christmas, when there were bills to be paid and spring orders in the factories. The picture may be very different elsewhere and should be checked so that there are at least a few calls soon after the service announces its opening.

FAMILIAR ARRANGEMENTS

The first few months of the service will probably provide the consultant many opportunities to encourage the Day Care Neighbor to widen her circle of neighborly interaction. It is predictable that the Day Care Neighbor will at first tend to make arrangements in the areas she is most familiar and comfortable with.

- If she has teenage children who are in demand as babysitters, she may try to meet calls that they cannot fill by finding other young babysitters and putting them in touch with the prospective users.

- If she has been a working mother in the recent past, she may have friends who continue to work and who turn to her for help in finding day care.
- If she is giving day care as a means of supplementing insufficient family income or providing some "extras" for her children, she may be most interested in meeting the needs of others in a similar position.

The consultant may also have the needs of special populations in mind—A.F.D.C.mothers trying to achieve financial independence, for example, or professional women in critically understaffed occupations.

The consultant can help Day Care Neighbors enlarge their view of those to be served by:

- describing some of the day care needs reported to the central office and asking the Day Care Neighbor's opinion (choosing situations outside the specific neighborhood to avoid the implication that the Day Care Neighbor is expected to take some action on them);
- asking questions about families described earlier in interviews or placed on the map;
- inquiring for additional information about previous arrangements—what do givers and users report about their experience?

An attitude of relaxed interest in what the Day Care Neighbor is already doing is more likely to stimulate speculation on her part about further possibilities than a more direct approach. And the "snowball" effect of her increased activity in the day care system—others' recognition that she can and will help—also serves to increase her awareness of need and broaden her range of activity.

Counseling

As noted, Day Care Neighbors not only help in making day care arrangements but also give advice about day care and other problems neighbors bring to them. As she becomes widely known, the Day Care Neighbor will be called on more and more for counseling. While in the past she has not been self-conscious about offering advice, she may now feel uncertain of her ability to give it in view of her more "official" role. The presence of the consultant may make her aware of her nonprofessional status. She may feel she is expected to refer requests for advice to the consultant, or tell the troubled person to contact the consultant.

This may at first pose a dilemma for the consultant. The problem presented may be quite serious and complex; the consultant's training and professional self-image may impel her to "take the case." She must recognize, however, that if she does, it will impair the colleague relationship—in fact nullify the whole service—since in a very short time she would have the kind of case load that leaves no time for consultation with Day Care Neighbors. The consultant should remind herself that the Day Care Neighbor was chosen for judgment and skill in carrying on human relations and for her position close to those needing help.

We found that if we met a request for our intervention with questions about the Day Care Neighbor's views of the situation, the Day Care Neighbor quickly recognized that she was able to handle the situation herself—and so did we. The Day Care Neighbor's advice was sometimes different from what we would have given—which particular form of discipline for a disturbed child, or how to resolve a marital problem—but it was usually well suited to the situation and culture of the particular neighborhood.

We noted, too, that Day Care Neighbors were keen observers of behavior and capable of sophisticated interpretations of it. They made use of their natural abilities and interests and had often augmented these with courses on child development or reading in the mass media.

We had originally planned that where agency referrals seemed indicated, we would take over and make the referral. We found, it was more successful, however, if we made only the initial contact with the agency and then put the agency and Day Care Neighbor in direct contact with each other. This conserved the time and energy of all involved, gave the agency a firsthand insight into the situation, and maintained the Day Care Neighbor in the central position appropriate for her.

The Day Care Neighbor was an invaluable link in an agency referral since she was in the position of helping the troubled person make the contact, offering encouragement and support for its duration and after termination. In the occasional situations where, after talking it over with the Day Care Neighbor, we took a more active role in the referral and follow-through, the Day Care Neighbor was kept informed of what was happening.

Operating the Service: Carrying Through

Building a Firm Partnership

It might be assumed that when Day Care Neighbors are functioning well in an increasingly widening system, the consultant will have little more to do than collect statistics. In fact, however, as Day Care Neighbors receive requests from increasing numbers of givers and users who find them through word of mouth, the problems inherent in family day care and in the daily lives of young families become more evident. Inability to provide service is especially threatening to Day Care Neighbors, sensitive to the feelings of all involved and feeling responsible for assuring a successful outcome.

SPACING INTERVIEWS

The first few meetings between the Day Care Neighbor and the consultant should be set by the consultant in a matter of fact manner at the convenience of the Day Care Neighbor. Weekly intervals appear to be desirable at first. When a relationship has been established between them and the Day Care Neighbor appears to feel reasonably secure in carrying on her activities, the consultant may then suggest that interviews be more widely spaced and finally set at monthly intervals at a mutually convenient regular time.

THE DAY CARE NEIGHBOR'S DEPENDENCE

It may be surprising to discover that a Day Care Neighbor who at first forgot appointments or found it difficult to fit contacts with the consultant into her busy life may eventually resist having less contact. But as the Day Care Neighbor becomes more conscious of her role, she may also feel greater responsibility for doing the job adequately. She may feel she cannot do it without the consultant's help even though she has virtually done so for years without help from anyone. The consultant, by stressing her availability at any time for a personal visit or telephone conversation, can quickly restore the Day Care Neighbor's self-confidence. It is important for the consultant to emphasize:

- the Day Care Neighbor's greater competence than the consultant's to function in the neighborhood day care system (not as the person who is there to save the time of the consultant or substitute for her);
- the consultant's ongoing interest and concern with whatever interests or concerns the Day Care Neighbor in the day care system;
- the consultant's availability as liaison with community resources.

THE CONSULTANT-DAY CARE NEIGHBOR PARTNERSHIP

The relationship between the social work consultant and the Day Care Neighbor:

- sustains the Day Care Neighbor and supports her through many frustrating, unrewarding encounters in the day care system;
- provides a model for the Day Care Neighbor to follow in her relationship with givers and users with whom she may have difficulty;
- is the instrument for changing attitudes that may inhibit the Day Care Neighbor's functioning.

The consultant is responsible for maintaining the relationship at a level and in a manner that will be of greatest value to the Day Care Neighbor. The consultant must make some estimate of the Day Care Neighbor's characteristics, her attitude toward herself and others. The depth and sophistication of this estimate will depend on the degree of the consultant's professional training, but every consultant must put much thought and planning into building a relationship with every Day Care Neighbor. The relationship should be reviewed from time to time as it changes. Unlike therapeutic relationships, however, it is not discussed between them except in strict reality terms.

CHARACTERISTIC DAY CARE NEIGHBOR ATTITUDES

Like everyone else, the Day Care Neighbors' attitudes were influenced by their culture and inner development. Many were feeling conflicts between their personal preference for staying at home and the socially devalued position of being "only a housewife," between their belief that their children would develop best if they did not go out to work and a wish to provide the "extras" their work might earn. In addition, it seemed to us that most Day Care Neighbors were:

- at a time when their children no longer needed their full-time attention;
- interested in helping others and unsure of their skills in this area. This was especially true of the more privileged Day Care Neighbors who had professional friends and acquaintances and contrasted professional training with their own lack of it;
- at a stage in their own lives which recalled and reactivated some elements in their earlier experience.

In general, we found little difference according to socioeconomic level in the Day Care Neighbors' attitudes toward themselves. There were some, but not very marked, differences in their attitudes toward others. All of the Day Care Neighbors were:

- more interested and sympathetic with working mothers whose circumstances required them to go to work than with mothers who did not "need" to work;
- responsive to requests for help in emergencies and crises and willing to explore new resources;
- inclined toward stereotyped judgment of groups as divorcees or welfare recipients;
- unwilling generally to follow up on the outcome of arrangements. Although some Day Care Neighbors planned a follow-up, few actually did it, probably because they viewed it as an intrusion, a nosiness they considered destructive gossiping.

Bringing About Change. The consultant, as noted previously, does *not* attempt to effect major personality change in the Day Care Neighbor, nor to "teach" her. If Day Care Neighbors have been well selected, the task of the consultant will be chiefly to convey to them that:

- they do make an important contribution to the community as well as to their families in their roles as Day Care Neighbors;
- they are contributing to the development of a vital, new kind of child welfare service;
- the efforts of welfare recipients to cope with the harsh and narrow alternatives open to single mothers may lead to behavior condemned by the general public but understandable to those who want to help them;
- deeply troubled givers or users may behave in demanding and unreasonable ways.

Although the consultant will not expect to change the Day Care Neighbor's character, her relationships within her own family, or her lifestyle, some changes may occur as a result of the continuing partnership. The consultant should avoid direct discussion of the Day Care Neighbor's personality, even if she seems to invite it, since this would create a client-worker relationship. The consultant may make use of the same techniques adopted in earliest interviews when the Day Care Neighbor talked about her children and other aspects of her personal life. The consultant may:

- be an interested listener;
- use what she hears to increase her own understanding of the Day Care Neighbor and her system;
- make friendly comments;
- avoid judgmental or therapeutically oriented statements.

The consultant may find some changes occurring in her own attitudes. She may develop:

- greater acceptance for lay people she may previously have seen as punitive—insensitive to the clients she works with;
- a stronger appreciation of community interaction and its potential for support, rarely apparent from a social-agency base;
- more flexibility in accepting problem-solving approaches radically different from those of her profession;
- new insights into the day care system that may, in turn, be used

both to adapt the service to fit the particular needs of certain neighborhoods and as the basis for social-service planning in general.

As the relationship between the Day Care Neighbor and the consultant grows, both will move forward with increased assurance of their place and function in the partnership.

HELPING DAY CARE NEIGHBORS WITH MAINTENANCE PROBLEMS

"Maintenance" involves all activities directed toward stabilizing, supporting, and improving the relationship between the user and giver of day care.

Maintenance Difficulties. Day Care Neighbors find maintenance activities harder than recruitment and matching because:

- they have had least experience with maintenance. In the informal day care system when a suggestion is made, its outcome is not followed up; in fact, it is considered "none of my business" even to inquire if an arrangement was made;
- an active and sometimes aggressive approach is needed just to get answers to the simpler maintenance questions;
- they see the role as snooping into the affairs of others and fear that givers and users may react negatively to inquiries about maintenance.

The consultants may find it difficult to help Day Care Neighbors in maintenance activities because the consultants may:

- believe the Day Care Neighbor ought to be able to manage these matters successfully after the relatively long period of preparation;
- view maintenance tasks as really the province of professionals;
- find continuing contacts with Day Care Neighbors to be somewhat dull and repetitious.

If a firm relationship has been established between the consultant and Day Care Neighbor, however, none of these considerations will prevent them both from recognizing the need for maintenance activity and moving toward meeting it. But even an excellent relationship will not insulate the Day Care Neighbor against some of the difficulties. They may be common and predictable, misunderstandings about payment and hours of care, which may be thinly veiled expressions of deeper dissatisfaction.

Even in the following case, which seemed satisfactory to everyone and a source of pride in making a fine arrangement to the Day Care Neighbor, complications occurred needing tactful handling to preserve an essentially positive arrangement for a little girl who needed it and for the two adults involved. Angry termination might have had a bad effect on future arrangements.

12/16

DCN: Patty was telling me Terry's mother hadn't paid her for a month and she doesn't know what to do.

SWC: Does she usually pay by the week?

DCN: I don't know. Patty said when she first started with her, she asked her if it would be all right if she didn't pay her every week. Patty said, "Yes, I don't care." But it's gone on about a month now and Patty said, "I kind of worry about her." She asked Patty over to see her new apartment and Patty said, "It's real nice, but I just kind of had the feeling that there's a lot of things she wants on her income, you know, and that maybe she's getting herself, you know . . ." And Patty says that the other thing is that Terry does come a little earlier now in the mornings. And Patty says she didn't really arrange to give Terry breakfast. You know, the mother was going to give her breakfast and then send her around, but Patty says now usually her family is eating and she says, "Terry, come on, did you eat your breakfast this morning?" And Terry says, "No, I didn't have any breakfast." So, Patty says, "She'll always sit right down and eat" . . .

Patty said, "I'm just worried that maybe her mother takes on too much, financially as well as doing too much. She kind of forgets things. Like, I told her Ben and I would be gone over Thanksgiving—I told her a long time ago, you know, weeks before, that I wouldn't be in town the Friday after Thanksgiving, and wouldn't be there Wednesday afternoon." . . . Terry's mother didn't say too much . . ." When I told her, oh, I think Monday or Tuesday night, 'You know I won't be here . . . till Monday,' you know, she looked at me with a blank look like she'd never heard the story before." And Patty said, "Gee, I thought it was so funny because I'd gone all over it with her. . . . I can't think about what could have happened unless it was that she had her mind on something else over there." So the mother said to Patty, sort of mad, she said, "Well, I don't know what I'll do. I'll have to take the day off." . . .

6/10

DCN: Patty says she's not going to keep Terry when school's first out this summer.... Her kids will all be home and will want a lot of her time and attention and anyway she thinks it's time Terry's mother took a little more responsibility for her. Patty suggested she send her to day camp—it will be a good preparation for school next fall. She said to me, "The mother just acted like it was really none of my business. She'll find a situation for herself and on and on and on." Patty said she didn't think she'd ever do it. Patty said, "Her grandparents came to pick Terry up one day. They're just exactly like the mother, you know—you could just tell that they're not too concerned about her. They just take care of her, but that's about it."

I said I didn't blame Patty, but I sure thought Terry would have a tough summer and then to start school ... they say that is real hard for kids who don't feel too secure at home. So then Patty said, "I suppose when it doesn't work out right that I'll take her back over here, but," she says, "I just wanted her mother to see if she could make some arrangement. But I'm not going to take it out on Terry even if her mother is more of a kid than Terry is!"

There may be crises to which Day Care Neighbors respond without any reward of any kind.

DCN: Oh, I'm just disgusted and embarrassed too. A girl called, said she knew my daughter from work and would I please help her or she'd lose her job and have to go on welfare. Seems her babysitter quit, and she had no place to leave her six-months-old baby, but I couldn't take her—I've got all I'm allowed. So I called my neighbor and she said she'd be willing to help her, but she gave her crib away just last month. Well, so we both ran all over the place till we found a crib to borrow and she was all set early today for the baby—and the girl never showed or called up or anything. And I really don't know my neighbor all that well and I think she is awfully mad at me and maybe thinks I was fooling her or something. I could kill that girl and wait till I talk to my daughter about recommending me to people like that!

Evidence of Maintenance Problems. If the relationship between the Day Care neighbor and consultant is well established, the Day Care Neighbor will turn to the consultant for support (as happened in the examples above), usually with a telephone call almost immediately after a disturbing event. But some Day Care Neighbors who have very high standards for themselves may not take such a direct approach. It may well be they cannot admit, even to themselves, how upset they are. We found when Day Care Neighbors talked about going to work or otherwise implied terminating participation in the Day Care Neighbor Service, they often had had an upsetting maintenance problem.

A consultant will have to consider the reasons for a Day Care Neighbor's sudden decision to go to work. She may express regret at the prospect of losing the Day Care Neighbor. A comment about the difficulties of the Day Care Neighbor's work and its importance and value may also be in order. It may be useful to point out that Day Care Neighbor work has little public visibility and much that is frustrating. If the consultant considers it best to deal more openly with the underlying problem, she may, of course, inquire directly whether there has been some unusually upsetting incident.

In every case, the consultant should:

- avoid cross-examining in an effort to separate facts from feelings. Fixing blame serves no useful purpose and arouses needless defensiveness.
- support the Day Care Neighbor's handling of similar matters in the past and her ability to do so in the future.
- give reasons why givers or users have behaved in unreasonable and inconsiderate ways without making psychological "excuses" for them.

We found that difficulties between users and givers resulted from a relatively narrow range of causes:

- an unexpected change in life pattern—a sudden move, the appearance of a "free babysitter," physical or mental illness, marital discord;
- the day care giver (or user) was identified with a person who was disliked, feared, or otherwise found lacking;
- financial embarrassment due to poor budgeting, impulse buying, or more pressing need.

When these possibilities for otherwise unreasonable behavior were suggested to Day Care Neighbors, they were often able to recognize and accept them. We avoided giving psychologically detailed diagnoses since the purpose was to help the Day Care

Neighbor help the giver and user, not to turn her into a psychotherapist.

NEGLECT AND ABUSE

Perhaps the most trying situations involve a Day Care Neighbor's awareness of the neglect or abuse of a child, by his own family or the day care giver. The conflict between providing immediate protection for the child and refraining from false accusations against the adults is keenly felt by professionals; it is even more painful for Day Care Neighbors who may have friendly relationships with those they now see as guilty of serious offenses against children. But one of the major assets of the service is that Day Care Neighbors, because of their community position, may learn of neglect or abuse long before it comes to the attention of official agencies.

When the Day Care Neighbor describes such a situation, the consultant will want to act quickly to protect the child and should offer to intervene herself, make a referral to a protective agency, or urge the Day Care Neighbor do so. In spite of the urgency, however, the consultant should remember that more may be gained for everyone if the Day Care Neighbor is helped to take action herself, even if it is somewhat delayed by her initial reluctance. Here, as elsewhere, the strength of the relationship of trust built up between consultant and Day Care Neighbor will help them both deal wisely with these very explosive problems.

We found it *was* possible for Day Care Neighbors to take appropriate action, even when the neglecting mother was a personal friend, if we were patient, accepted her ambivalence, and focused on the importance of the contribution she could make for the welfare of the whole family.

The consultant will probably have no direct way of determining whether she is succeeding in increasing the maintenance activities of the Day Care Neighbor. So many reality factors affect outcome that improvement cannot easily be estimated by statistical methods, but a few indications may be useful signs. The Day Care Neighbor may:

- explain behavior in a new problem arrangement in language used by the consultant in a previous one;

- telephone to say "I tried what you said and it worked";
- describe her own variation on something the consultant suggested with the confidence of a full partner and friend;
- demonstrate and even discuss a shift in her point of view from judgmental to more accepting.

Dealing with Other Problems

REQUESTS FROM UNSUITABLE USERS AND GIVERS

It's more difficult for both consultant and Day Care Neighbor to know how to deal with the occasional instance when it's clear that those wanting an arrangement are not suitable. Often these are people subject to severe emotional and financial drain and under much pressure to find children to care for or have their children cared for. Such problem day care givers may be:

- women without marketable skills in dire need of immediate income;
- childless women and others who seek companionship from a child as a kind of household pet;
- women with a "rescue fantasy," a belief that all parents are neglecting and incompetent and that only they can offer children what they need;
- women who see child care as an easy way of making money.

Day care users likely to pose problems may be:

- women known for exploiting day care givers by failing to pay and keeping irregular hours;
- women who even on brief contact are seen to have little understanding of the needs of their children;
- women whose income is so marginal it is obvious they cannot hope to pay for child care but will lose even marginal income if they cannot make an arrangement.

A Day Care Neighbor in a large apartment house said:

Mae downstairs [in the apartment house], she's mad at me because she wants to babysit and and I don't send her any of the kids I don't take. She was working and only paying two-fifty for her two kids a day and she couldn't get a sitter and now she's staying home and wants me to find her some kids to sit for. So she's up here every day—"Found anybody yet?" And I told her, "Please stay off my back." I'm not going to give her the names of any babies. She's asked for babies but she's too . . . now with older kids, maybe. She's just got her whole life built around her own. Everybody has to give in to them or she gets angry. But you put a little one in there—I think babies need the most loving, you know—and she can't be bothered. She'd give them a sandwich or a cookie, you know, but I don't think she's the kind could love a baby. I might be wrong, but I've just got that feeling . . . until it changes, I won't find her anyone no matter how much she bugs me.

These situations are distressing to Day Care Neighbors—and perhaps no less to consultants. Few of them are met in any other agency practice. It is a major asset of the Day Care Neighbor Service that they do appear and become of concern. In some instances the consultant may encourage the Day Care Neighbor to carry on counseling and referral activities on their behalf. An old lady who should not be caring for young children, for example, may well be in demand to sit with an older person and can be put in touch with an agency providing such a service; a young woman user on marginal income may be referred to an agency for vocational training or child care subsidy.

The Day Care Neighbor is often well aware of licensing laws and has her own commitment to recommending only those who abide by them. Reporting license violations may be dealt with in the same way as neglect cases described above.

THE DAY CARE NEIGHBOR'S ROLE IN TERMINATING CARE

While Day Care Neighbors can be expected to make excellent judgments about care in advance, they are no more infallible than professionals. It's possible that an arrangement they helped make will be seen as unsuitable by one of the parties to it. The consultant will deal with this situation as with recruitment failures. If there are a number of such situations involving one Day Care Neighbor, the consultant will wish to review them and determine whether they are attributable to problems in the neighborhood or other external influences or to some personality problem of the Day Care

Neighbor. In our experience, Day Care Neighbors proved most tactful and resourceful in discouraging poor arrangements and avoiding making them.

TERMINATION OF DAY CARE NEIGHBORS BY CHOICE

We can only speculate about the natural time span Day Care Neighbors will remain in the service since our service lasted four years and none withdrew from choice. Theoretically, it seems likely that Day Care Neighbors would want to terminate when circumstances in their own lives change—children leave the home, the family moves out of the neighborhood, new interests and demands take their time. The consultant will be careful not to cut off the relationship abruptly, as though the Day Care Neighbor was "deserting," but will taper it off, as happens with friends who may gradually see less and less of each other as the circumstances of their lives change and separate them.

Three of our Day Care Neighbors terminated because their husbands were forced to move to new jobs. Two remained in touch with us by mail and reported efforts to organize Day Care Neighbor Services in their new communities.

Two Day Care Neighbors moved within the city and were anxious to continue in the service. One remained working in her former neighborhood and social system. The other moved into an entirely new neighborhood establishing herself as a Day Care Neighbor in amazingly brief time.

DISCONTINUING USE OF A DAY CARE NEIGHBOR

It may be necessary to end a Day Care Neighbor's contact with the service because she is unsuited to her role. This is unquestionably difficult because:

- professional responsibility requires that it be carried out without implication of blame;
- the consultant must avoid projecting her own failure in discrimination onto the Day Care Neighbor;
- it will be difficult to recruit another Day Care Neighbor in the same area without injury to the person terminated.

Using Additional Communication Avenues

SENSE OF BELONGING

Day Care Neighbors, relatively isolated from each other because they're selected according to their position in their respective neighborhoods, may miss the support and stimulation of sharing experiences with others in the same job. Since contact with the central service may be limited to the relationship with the consultant colleague, they do not have the support and esprit de corps that membership in a respected community service often offers. Here, membership in Associations may fill a real need for them, and they with their wider perspectives of givers and users—and consultants—may have major contributions to make to the scope and stability of an Association.

Bulletin or Newsletter. We developed a bulletin which we sent to Day Care Neighbors monthly as an extension of the colleague relationship. We hoped it would:

- give day Care Neighbors a sense of belonging to an organization;
- provide a permanent reference resource;
- reflect current concerns common to the Day Care Neighbors, as perceived by the consultant in individual sessions;
- describe anonymously the manner in which individual Day Care Neighbors have coped with these problems;
- describe or give brief abstracts of materials on child care otherwise not available to Day Care Neighbors (avoiding the obvious that can be found in all mass media);
- avoid personalities and reports of minor personal events, but focus on the Day Care Neighbor role and minimize competition between Day Care Neighbors.

It wasn't easy to produce a monthly bulletin, but the Day Care Neighbors seemed to find it useful at times in allaying their anxieties and broadening understanding of difficult situations. We were pleased when Day Care Neighbors incorporated concepts from the bulletins into their practice. Some shared copies with friends and neighbors.

Reaching the Community

As Day Care Neighbors reach out toward users and givers, they touch ever widening social systems. They have opportunities to describe the service to interested groups. Through these appearances they make new contacts and gain status. Wherever practical, consultants should encourage them to take on such tasks, even if the original invitation comes to the consultant.

For us, an unanticipated consequence of their activities was their new understanding of social problems in general and those affecting working mothers in particular. Several of the upper- and middle-class Day Care Neighbors described finding that they had an almost evangelical zeal when they talked about their new attitudes and knowledge with their friends. They also became active in promoting legislation and other needed changes.

DCN: I was thinking when I... the other day when we were at the restaurant after the show and I went to make a phone call to see if our babysitter was doing all right with the children, I had to wait for the phone to be free. The phone is in the cocktail lounge, and the cocktail hostess was desperately using the phone in great anxiety, talking to *her* babysitter——

SWC: She was talking to her babysitter?

DCN: Begging her to stay longer since *she* had to stay longer at the restaurant—"Well, can your sister come if you can't stay?" You know, you could just see that poor working woman... it was by then ten or eleven—she said it might be two or three in the morning before she could leave. I just felt so sorry for her, because this is what the Day Care Neighbor Service does partly. I never before would have thought of the cocktail hostess even having children. It wouldn't have occurred to me. And probably most of these women do. They are too old to be young unmarried girls. They are women who have already been divorced or, you know, somehow have to support children. I was mad at myself that I didn't say, "Call me tomorrow and maybe I can help you make a better arrangement."

The Day Care Neighbor Service and the Future

We were disappointed that after favorable reception of the original Day Care Neighbor Service Handbook—the volume of requests alone seemed to indicate a widespread interest in replication—we did not have to fight off the flattery of imitation. Formal and informal inquiries about the experiences of those making practical use of the handbook led us to conclude that though some found it an interesting possibility, few had tried it. We were no doubt naive to suppose that it would be quickly adopted, but we had watched demonstration results of other projects (some of which we thought considerably less well founded than ours) being adopted nationally almost as fast as the paper dried, though not necessarily with success.

As we corresponded and talked with people across the country, professionals in particular, we sought to learn the reasons for this paradoxical situation where there was such a positive, interested response to this new, financially feasible, professionally uncomplicated service, and yet lack of replication to test out its validity elsewhere.

One of our first findings was that we were wrong—that indeed our concepts had been seriously considered and partly incorporated into a variety of programs and discussed as an alternative form of family day care service delivery in official and unofficial journals. Some public programs with considerable impact have made use of the geographic aspect of the service as a newer way of providing family day care. The "systems" usually have a core of consultants, specialists in nutrition and early-childhood education, who either visit the homes of the day care giver regularly or are available on call, rather than using the Day Care Neighbor between the consultant and the recipients of service.

We recognized that the major stumbling block toward the development of Day Care Neighbor Services was the difficulty professionals had in understanding and accepting the concept that Day Care Neighbors existed—that they didn't have to be created or trained in the conventional way; that their judgment of the quality and appropriateness of a family day care arrangement was as good as—or often a good deal better than—that of professionals who could not be the close and continuing observers Day Care Neighbors were. There seemed to be a belief, too, that none but professionals could act as resources to givers and users in making good arrangements for their children, or suggesting constructive and interesting play materials or menus or even first-aid measures, attitudes which seemed to ignore the general level of information open to all through the mass media.

It was likely, too, that in their enthusiasm to try some of the ideas of the Day Care Neighbor Service some professionals "came on too strong," with the predictable result of causing the Day Care Neighbors to withdraw instead of becoming partners.

The Director of a project adapting the Day Care Neighbors as we described it to a special setting in a very creative manner commented:

I just had a conference with two of the consultants and we were talking about a meeting that some of the Day Care Neighbors were having over there tomorrow night. They said they weren't planning to go: "It has nothing to do with us... they know as much as we do... whatever they want is okay. It's up to them—if they need us they'll let us know." I said I didn't agree with that and then they said, "Well, really, we don't know anything more than the parents. We're parents, too, and we haven't all the answers."

Well, that isn't true, it's obviously not true, and I began to talk to them about what they know and what it could mean if they could act like partners instead of sort of pals. And then I realized that they really had a need not to see themselves as different and apart because they're mostly white or at least middle-class and the Day Care Neighbors are poor and black. I guess I like it better that they feel this way than the way it might have been ten years ago when they barged in and gave orders, but I'm going to have to find some way of getting them to a place somewhere in between.

The role of consultant seems to be a troubling one, perhaps because it has been developed and chiefly employed under mental-health auspices and so is not familiar as a method to many professionals in other fields of service. In discussing a project undertaking to replicate the field study of the neighborhood family day care system the director asked:

What core of knowledge or skills should the consultant have? Is it a discipline or a set of learning? Are we simply saying that we'll move the professionalization component back a little but there is something you must go through to do this? We've been favoring, I think, people with early childhood education and maybe we would do better to concentrate more on the adult.

A secondary use for a Day Care Neighbor Service that seemed significant emerged only as the writers became involved in the problems of information and referral services; it may now prove to be the avenue through which professionals and Day Care Neighbors will form productive partnerships. As information and referral services become better known in a community and the volume of requests threatens to outstrip the possibilities of adding space and staff, these services will inevitably come into contact with people they may recognize as acting as Day Care Neighbors in their neighborhoods. It may be useful to assign some information and referral service staff some time to act as consultants to these natural community-resource people whose activities will be enhanced when they can make use of the resources of a citywide service and can, in turn, help the central service offer the quality that comes only from firsthand acquaintance with neighborhoods and their people—the natural province of the Day Care Neighbors.

We feel that a Day Care Neighbor Service could be attached also to day care centers, schools, mental health clinics, and welfare agencies where public and private services could and would complement each other.

CHAPTER 7

LICENSING

The Stormy Emergence of Licensing

Two procedures traditionally confined to agency-sponsored day care—licensing and training—are now becoming important to informal day care, adding another link to bonds bringing the two approaches to family day care into closer, more productive contact. Their relationship is somewhat stormy as yet, perhaps more of an armistice than an alliance, while terms for coexistence are negotiated. To understand what is at issue requires a quick survey of the past.

Licensure is a procedure for assuring the public that certain standards experts consider essential to safe, healthy, and competent operation are being met. The site, plant, and personnel must meet these standards before a special service can be offered. Failure to comply with licensing regulations usually carries a legal penalty, ranging from an order to desist to fines and more drastic measures.

When group care facilities were first organized, it was tacitly assumed that their benevolent sponsors would assure that they were safely operated. But it soon became clear that the same pressures that led to the development of charitable day nurseries also stimulated private individuals to offer day nursery care. Since they did so in an effort to earn money, and therefore took as many children as they could crowd in, and saved all they could on food, these "baby farms" were soon notorious for neglect that was life-threatening to infants crowded into them. Licensure was one way of combating these shoddy operations. Day nurseries were soon required to meet licensing regulations which, since chiefly addressed to health conditions and fire safety, were often vested in health or fire departments and sometimes in both.

Home day care for children, probably because so often given by a relative with no money exchanged, was very rarely considered in licensing regulations although there were some isolated localities where standards were set but only enforced when flagrantly breached and injury to children came to public notice.

The picture changed with the infusion of large sums of public money, for two reasons. The need for accountability required reasonable assurance to granting bodies that the funds were allocated for the benefit of children and in no way underwrote poor care but contributed to a higher standard of care. The leverage of federal money was also seen as encouraging improvement of existing care by making licensure a condition of receipt. In many optimistic plans for wider use of licensing, the licensor was seen to have a unique entree into family day care homes, which might accept the licensing inspector as an adviser and educator as well as a person who could assure that only homes which were of acceptable quality would care for young children.

The first of the new licensing regulations, though often accepting this utopian view, were modeled on regulations from the past, chiefly on physical safety and health aspects of care. In many instances existing regulations for day nurseries were simply transferred to family day care homes. The federal government encouraged licensing bodies to include public child welfare personnel in drafting licensing regulations, and further to house the regulating authority in a public welfare facility that, in most instances, already had the licensing authority for foster home care. Licensing officials soon discovered they had reckoned without considering the reaction of caregivers who had, for years, been independent operators.

A public official in the day care department of a children's services agency said:

The law requires everyone to be licensed and many more have been licensed this year than ever before. It's much more acceptable, more known, and people are finding it isn't so bad. We still have a lot of unlicensed care, of course, partly because they don't know how to go about it. It's hard to do, they think, and very restrictive. Some say, "I don't choose to obey this particular law." The licensing units' job has just multiplied. Our county departments are also getting more comfortable with regulatory responsibility, so they're more alert and ready to follow up on ads of people who are not licensed.

A licensor said:

I do spot checks on the homes the regular workers have approved for day care. They don't always keep me up to date, so when I get to the home, sometimes there have been changes—this child has been withdrawn, this day care mother withdrew, this one has moved, this child has been transferred to another home. Spot-checking means I go in without any warning, but I want the person to feel at ease when I'm there. (She knows I'm coming sometime.) I usually go in in the morning unless I'm concerned about the afternoon program or what kind of food they provide. The things I ask . . . like, if there are pets, I ask, "Did they have their shots?" I look around for safety. Some of them think you're there to spy on them, and I guess I am. Sometimes I wish I was a worker within an agency where I had twenty to twenty-five homes to be responsible for. Finding new homes, encouraging them to take courses, is what I'd love to do but I can't do that. I just go in, the obvious is there, and that's what I report on.

Problems and Pitfalls of Licensing

People responsible for licensing judgments soon saw that the excellence of a family day care home depended heavily on the role and character of the giver and that it was therefore important to consider these factors in determining who received licenses. But, as in foster care, there seemed no way of defining or measuring the essential personal qualities. In fact, it was nearly impossible to define those qualities even where there was general agreement about whether abilities to keep a clean, safe home, cooperate with a central social agency, keep accurate records, and provide good meals were essentials of good care. Should compatibility with young children be included, and even the ability to be supportive and cooperative with parents? Should family day care givers be chosen for their educational attainments, their ability to learn how to teach young children, for their warmth, willingness to discipline with firmness and humor, affection for young children? These issues and others they raised were furiously debated within and without licensing agencies, child welfare agencies (public and private) and by prospective licensees. All were acquainted with excellent physical facilities that were cold, unfriendly places where young children might suffer emotional, if not physical, harm. And all knew the opposite situation—a less than desirable structure, not scrupulously clean, where a talented and interested family day care giver provided affection, appropriate stimulation, and attention under which children blossomed to the satisfaction of their grateful parents.

If standards to be set were those that could be objectively measured, then it would be relatively easy to train licensors, to count doors and windows and estimate cubic feet of floor space in a day care home. But it was usually held that it took considerable professional training to make judgments about the personality traits of a stranger, even with the aid of objective instruments of personality measurement (not accessible to licensors). At first it seemed that it would be necessary to use highly trained people, but this idea was soon seen as not feasible in view of the enormity of the task and the limited funds allocated to a function that did not increase the numbers of day care homes as funds for direct subsidy were expected to do.

A licensor discusses some early experiences organizing a licensing unit:

The licensing position has been shuffled around . . . I've been through every supervisor in the last three years. . . .

The licensing unit doesn't fit under a children's unit or an adult unit or a protective service unit, so frankly, I was lucky enough never to be involved with a whole unit and in that way I had more freedom to maneuver the position the way I felt it should go. I was free to say, "This is what I feel the priorities are, and this is how I'd like to do it"—if I could convince my supervisor at that time. I was hired because someone said, "Throw out the civil-service list and send me someone with some day care experience." Frankly, I didn't have a whole lot of day care experience, but if You're going to get into it, and that's what you're going to work at (and I knew more about it than anyone else, so they were willing to take my word for it) you learn, and I was willing to listen to some other people who knew a lot more about it than I did.

Most licensing regulations were intended to apply to everyone in a community who gave care, on the sound assumption that family day care was now widely in use at every socio-economic level and should be uniformly excellent for all young children. But the extent of use had rarely been estimated correctly since few public officials had had firsthand contact with the private family day care sector.

Licensing

Simply to make one visit to every day care home in a city would require a staff far beyond any estimates. And if the staff were highly trained professionals, the licensing function might consume most of the funds earmarked for subsidy. Add to this already impossible situation the transitory character of family day care. Arrangements could not be expected to endure over time as in much day nursery care. Both giver and user families in most arrangements were young and mobile. They changed residence often and entered and withdrew from the arrangements in response to changing work conditions, the pregnancy of giver or user, divorce and marriage, not to mention illness. Licensors spent a great deal of time on wild-goose chases.

But perhaps most inhibiting was the attitude of private family day care givers toward licensing, which not infrequently expressed itself against any licensor brave enough to attempt a home visit. It was undoubtedly true that family day care givers were often unreasonable in their resentment against individual licensors and the concept of licensing itself—they needed no one to tell *them* how to give good care.

A health educator in a county health department describes the difficulties he sees:

I studied at the University Child Development Center for a while and I taught young children before that, and my wife has been doing day care at home last year and this year. Now one of my goals is to get the health departments in three counties committed, or at least informed about what day care is.

Two weeks ago the licensing person came to our house—I told you my wife gives day care and we have a couple of small children of our own—and noticed our back porch, which she considered not safe because there was no guardrail. It's about two feet off the back lawn, and she wanted a railing. So I had to go to this outrageous junkyard and buy the outrageous wrought iron fencing. Now the top of it will be six feet off the ground and when the kids climb up on that and fall off, they could really get hurt. I guess we'll just have to wait for it to happen and then we can take it down.

A licensed day care giver said:

Every licensed day care giver I know knows people doing it who aren't licensed—they just don't want to hassle with it. A friend of mine gives great care and she always has more kids than she can take, but she won't get licensed—partly because of the money, but mostly the physicals and all that. She says it's ridiculous all of a sudden, she has to turn into a pro or something. She isn't going to do it.

A child advocacy expert remarked:

There's a real good reason why a lot of people on welfare give care without getting licensed in this town—if you're pregnant, you can't be licensed; if you have unrelated boarders in your home, you can't be licensed. And you and your husband have to be fingerprinted and interviewed at the department of social service. If your husband works, he has to take time off to do that—and he might just have a court record for petty theft or something that wouldn't make him want to do that—or talk about his childhood for two hours with a license worker. And it costs fifty dollars. It seems to me the licensing authorities are making people pay them to enforce rules that will preclude those same people from operating, or risk punishment. That's pretty far out.

Positive Results of Licensing Efforts

There are two major results of most licensing efforts. In the light of the reality of staff-home ratios, licensing became, either openly or tacitly, limited chiefly to homes receiving federal subsidy and those reported neglectful and those that advertised for children, thereby making their existence known to the licensing agency. In spite of a great deal of thought and the investment of much time and money, the ratio of licensed to unlicensed homes has not changed much from the ten percent to ninety percent figure noted in studies at the outset of the allocation of federal funds.

But the widely expanded efforts toward licensing have had some positive effects. One has already been noted—the establishment of lists of licensed givers and places people looking for licensed homes could call. This helped develop information and referral services and also demonstrated the needs and preferences of users and underscored the magnitude of the demand, not only by those "on welfare" but also by the many others in the private sector. It helped dispel the last vestiges of the old ideas that only the poor needed day care, or needed to give it to achieve independence, and that users were likely to make poor choices and therefore required a great deal of guidance.

An official of a private day care agency commented:

They did a study of supervised and unsupervised family day care and they found out it didn't make a significant difference at all. Usually parents make a fairly good judgment on who they're giving their child to. When you don't allow that, then you're really putting down parents. Unless there are real options, real selection, to criticize somebody for making a poor selection when there's nothing else available is ridiculous, given the pressures that people have to go to work.

There are a lot of givers who are licensed and are interested in learning more about activities, and some of them have more children than they can handle just because they're too nice—they take in one and before you know it, it's out of control and they don't know how to get rid of it so they can curtail. Some of them are abused. It's like a foster mother that an agency has that's real great—"Oh, she's so good, give her two retarded kids—Oh, she's really good, give her two disturbed kids—and before you know it . . .

Many licensors who had seen their job as objective inspection, a child-protective service, found themselves sympathetic and impressed with the skills day care givers demonstrated—the complicated interpersonal situations they dealt with; in many instances, their high degree of genuine interest, wisdom and skill in dealing with children and parents. They made use of this in helping establish Associations.

The licensor, although unquestionably sometimes seen as "hatchet man"—and sometimes deserving that title—often was the only person in the parent agency that day care givers came to really know and depend upon. The licensor had firsthand knowledge of the feasibility and acceptance of regulations, which could be reported back to the parent agency for possible change.

Licensors demonstrated daily to their superiors that the job assigned to them could not be done. No agency in the country would claim that its licensing operation does in fact do what it theoretically should do—assure that all family day care givers live up to a set of standards. Nowhere has sufficient licensing staff been funded to carry out the job as defined.

It is sometimes argued that a licensing law is still essential so that those found to be giving poor care may be prohibited from doing so. But few licensing laws carry a penalty for noncompliance other than the prohibition against public advertisement. Where there is a penalty, it is rarely imposed. And there is absolutely no evidence that day care givers who have been so penalized cease to give care.

There is no doubt that needy and inadequate givers and users find each other outside the licensing procedure, and that some of the children who most need good substitute care get care that is little better than that given by the legendary drunken neglecting neighbor. Perhaps if the best licensors were freed from routine inspection of already adequate to excellent homes, they might have time to seek out families that most need child care advice and help and learn how to help them toward child care arrangements having a truly positive effect on otherwise seriously endangered children.

In talking with many licensing officials and others across the country, we have heard of dissatisfaction with licensing regulations in many quarters. But, on the other hand, people are giving a great deal of thought to possible alternatives.

An official in a state day care program says:

The home had to be licensed before it could accept children, so we would often come in before there were any children in the home. We could see the house, see that there were two exits, but in terms of the type of care that was going to be given, it was very hard to determine. Our requirements were so vague, and still are so minimal, that virtually everyone that we visited met the requirements. There were a few over the years that we've come across that we've encouraged not to go further in the process and denied a license to, but in fact most people substantially complied with the requirements. So we were in a position of not getting a lot of information about the care and also going into a home that met the requirements already, and then asking them to wait six or eight weeks to get a license because we were too understaffed to do all the paperwork and get them physicals sooner. This is idiocy.

What we were doing was yielding us so little that the risk was worth it and we moved directly into registration. People are now being registered rather than licensed and that means they're evaluating themselves regarding requirements. It also gives us a chance to test the forms that we use. We found out very quickly that they were not good. We are in the process now of looking at them again, given the kinds of feedback we have gotten from people, to try to revise them and make them more workable. Meanwhile we were using our efforts in revising family day care regulations so that they looked like something that means something. I think there are several questions as to what the registration materials ought to look like. Some people who are not form-oriented or reading-oriented might say, "To Hell with it, I'm just not going to bother with it."

I don't know why, but intake jumped in one month with very little reaching out for new sources. People who called for licensing were informed of the change. The time of year we chose to switch is a busy time because children are going back to school and women are making their decisions for the coming school year, so our intake tends to be higher in the months of September and October anyway.

We were originally getting referrals solely through those newspapers that knew of us and were referring people who advertised to us for licensing. And that has begun to change. The other factor that I'm sure was instrumental in some parts of the state was the formation of the local council to this office. Those community groups did a lot of talking. The change allowed family day care staff to go out and begin to talk with other units of the office and I think we reached some people through that.

The stage we are in now is: revision of forms, the final revision of family day care requirements, and beginning movement into a public education program. The public education is a very important component to us, but we won't be prepared to fully launch it until we have new requirements and until we get additional people on staff. We will move into a system of strong encouragement to people to come and see us to get the information.

What I envision is a system where the registrar makes a swing through the region periodically and leaves material and information and is available on those days for people who want to come and talk with someone about "How do I go about doing this?" That has not happened yet and we'll see how that works. Within the next month we'll be training those registrars to do that job well—to talk with people, to explain the issues—how you go about getting registered—and also to begin to travel throughout the region, as well as to use the publicity within the office here.

Interestingly enough, people are coming to us, newspapers are coming to us. Something has happened and I'm not quite sure what it is. I think the timing is right for family day care. Newspapers want stories—before we had to go beg them not to take ads without having the person referred to us and now ... I really would have preferred that we didn't get involved in this until we could do it in a real organized way, but virtually every staff member I have has been approached by at least one newspaper asking for an article.

We're envisioning several other components to the program. Some are safeguards which really developed partly as a result of there not being that initial home visit. We'll be spot-checking the homes and, depending on what we find when we begin doing that, we'll either do more of it or less of it. I don't know what we're going to find when we begin looking at homes regularly.

We're also going to be making, as part of our public education program, a sort of statement to parents that we are here if you want to complain about the quality of care your child is getting. This will really be the first time this state, in family day care, has had anything like a formal complaint mechanism. It would be followed up and would be somewhat effective. We'll be addressing some of the materials we develop to parents and one of our requirements would be that family day care parents give parents a set of requirements to read so they'll be aware of what kind of things that a family day care provider, at least minimally, ought to do.

We'll be expanding and refining our referral service which is already operating. In each regional office there is a listing kept up to date of the family day care homes in that region so that people are encouraged to call that office for names. In addition to that we do a monthly mailing to any agencies or organizations that are interested in having this, and who do their own kind of referral around this area. I think we're going to have to do a great deal of public education about what registration means. Whenever we give out referrals over the phone, we tell people what it means to be registered and that they should understand the requirements are minimum in nature. Staff has really gotten excited about the change from licensing to registration—an attitude of "Wow, we've got a chance to do something," to grow and change themselves, to take on an additional role.

Licensors have often been a moving force in getting Associations organized and sustaining them. A state licensor explains:

I don't have the time to follow through on three or four visits like we'd like to and are regulated to do. We're just not staffed to do it. So I had to find some other vehicle that would accomplish what I was looking for—getting the day care mothers together, getting some initiative of their own going so you're not constantly having to drag each member individually into something. You just have to say the best way to do this is to forget about some other things.

And that was when I found Linda. She was a day care mother and she'd had a lot of early-childhood training and was active in neighborhood things and seemed to know everybody, and she was at home with her kids. So I talked to her a little about some of this and she just went ahead and she has a really great Association going. Once in a while she calls or we get together and talk about how to get something done—to help both or either of us—it isn't a one-way street. She can tell me a lot more about what the need is than I would ever know. They've even got started on setting up a referral service.

Some of the day care mothers, especially Linda, have been acting like one for a long time anyway.

All three of the new family day care services are being developed, almost without conscious recognition by the people involved—Linda appears to be a natural day care neighbor, who acts as an information and referral service in addition to being in close touch with other day care givers that seek her advice. And she has stimulated the formation of an Association. It is likely partnerships including "official" members from licensing and child care agencies of all kinds will find ways to modify licensing regulations, which are relatively inoperative, in favor of better ways of serving both givers and users.

CHAPTER 8

TRAINING

Teaching the Talented

When family day care began to be discussed as an alternative to center day care, the problem of accountability, as we have said, quickly became a crucial concern. It has been noted that most states had licensing regulations for day nurseries, assuring that tax money was spent only in physically acceptable facilities. In the rare instances in which licensing regulations appeared too minimal or were nonexistent, there were well-tried private foster care models on which to base improved standards. But this was not the case with family day care. In most states family day care for fewer than six children had not required licensing with its attendant problems of setting standards and enforcing them. But most difficult was the problem of determining the suitability of the giver, since it was now generally accepted that the quality of care depended quite heavily on this factor.

Given the enormous number of family day care homes and the frequent changes of arrangements, the fallacy of investing most of the funds for improved day care in a large staff of licensors was clear; the answer seemed to lie rather in an approach that had a long and venerable tradition in professional fields. In nursing and teaching, for example, as in medicine and the ministry, it was usually assumed that completion of a prescribed curriculum covering the knowledge essential to practice, assured the competence of the practitioner—earning him or her the "ticket of admission" to the circle of publicly approved practitioners. Training had always been a part of federally financed programs, and it appeared to be the clear answer to assuring that family day care was given by women who could do so competently. Strong pressures were brought to bear to devise licensing standards incorporating training requirements, and funds were allocated for training programs with curriculums that were seen as essential.

Since most family day care arrangements were made between users and givers without agency intervention, it was natural that users and givers loudly protested that they were as good or better judges of quality than busy licensors who often had no personal child care experience. It was hotly pointed out to legislative bodies attempting to draw up regulations that would bring in federal funds, that the essential personal qualities of warmth, humor, flexibility, which everyone agreed were needed in the care of young children, could not be mandated nor could their presence or absence be reliably judged by a hastily trained and overworked licensor "taught" in any formal training curriculum. In Chapter Five it was noted that these issues often acted as catalysts in organizing Associations. In most instances, legislative bodies understandably responded by including minimal personal requirements, leaving the emphasis on training.

Training programs had been developed in group care before the big push toward family care. Much work had been done preparing training materials and manuals; publications had been prepared on child development; health care and safety; nutritious meals; making toys and center equipment; and curriculum activities of all kinds. The curriculum was essentially based on the well-established program of training for nursery educators, but compressed into a shorter time span and with more emphasis on homemade equipment. Parents were often invited to help build equipment.

Family day care training programs adopted much of this material, some of it "as is," and some modified toward the specific uses of family day care givers as seen by training staff. Course-meeting times were often a problem for women who looked after their own and other people's children during the day and who were anxious to spend some time with their families in the evening—or were simply ready to forget about day care until next morning! Programs that began with a long period of theoretical instruction, no matter how professionally planned, bored day care givers—even those few who were reimbursed for attending. So most training courses became progressively shorter, focusing increasingly on subjects of special interest to family day care givers—relationships with mothers of the children in care, how to set and collect fees, how to deal with the response of your own children, what resources were available.

Some training experts discovered that brief workshops were preferred and more productive than conventional courses. Some tried a combination of training programs, with an eye toward establishing a plan attractive not only to day care givers obliged to attend to be reimbursed, but for others in the great majority who might be interested in day care now or in the future.

Training Programs That Work

A description of a number of these schemes with comments of those responsible for them follow. It is unfortunate that there have been no serious studies of preferences and detailed evaluation of training courses, except in the conventional surveys of responses by participants.

An educational expert describes an attempt in one new direction for training:

A couple of years ago several educators in the state got interested in the possibilities of family day care as an educational resource and got a grant to study it. We put together some materials and then began testing them. We have three field workers, each had a cluster of twelve day care mothers in a neighborhood and they worked with them one night a week for twelve weeks and also went into the homes and did an hour and a half visit once a week—bringing an activity, children's developmental materials, books—things like that. Now we've cut down to two months. We'd gotten a list of licensed mothers and written to say we would like to do this and get together to see what the needs and concerns were on which to build a twelve week program. I think that is the main difference between our program and many others—we do not have a curriculum, pretested. The first time the day care mothers gather, we make a list of the concerns they brainstorm. We have phase one, with weekly contacts, and then phase two, which is a follow-up. Here are the things which go on in the evening meeting weekly—what's done and who does it, and what the materials are, the home component and the work the day care mother does on her own, which can be anything from working on her ledger to reading a book in the library or trying out activities from the manual or anything else. The ledger is of her costs. If she's open to it, fine, but if she has a better system, fine. Same with other aspects—the field worker won't go in and say, "This week we'll read chapter so and so" or "Go to the library or some place for some recipes." Still, I think you must be firm in what your expectations are in order to keep a group meeting existing.

We've had welfare day care mothers in the same group with people who live in a fifty-thousand-dollar house. I think it works very well. We also have those who have been doing day care a long time along with those who have just begun and that's been helpful because they learn from each other. I'd say one of the other major components has been not only the day care mothers setting their own goal based on their needs as they perceive them, but also involving them in the leadership roles during the evening programs. In one group we had an R.N. who was a day care mother who did the health and safety component; another day care mother wrote a twelve-page handout on puppet making; one of the day care fathers did the first-aid, so sometimes we can even get the husbands involved.

Then in June each of the field workers began with a new neighborhood group and provided some follow-up with the first, roughly a third as much, so that each of the field workers was to have seen the day care mothers in the first group about four times rather than twelve during the next three-month block. Then in the fall they picked up a third group and ended their contact with the first. It was not written in the grant, but we have always tried to plug those people in the first group into the local Day Care Association and if there wasn't one, we'd help get one started.

I think the reason we got the first grant was that one of the purposes of the program was to demonstrate or find out whether or not welfare mothers could get off welfare by taking care of A.D.C. children and live happily ever after. What we learned was that there were very few situations where a mother who was on welfare and who is the only breadwinner in the family can make a go of it in family day care. They don't need any charts or graphs, though I made them. They know after doing it for two or three months that they're just running in place. So in our programs we have some A.D.C. mothers but very few and the reason is economic. There's no way they can make it and they know it. We have poor luck, too, in reaching unlicensed people—very, very poor. They just don't want to be identified because they are very suspicious of the program.

A training specialist describes her experience:

I try to get them to share their skills and resources with each other. In the group I'm working with now I'm having a difficult time because they're still checking each other out in the group.... they're very uncomfortable in this kind of arrangement. I'm not sure why.

We're having a workshop Monday night and people have been telling me in the homes, "I just want to talk." I think the mistake we made with this group is that we scheduled them too tight—we did the financial end, the growth and development and discipline, and we didn't allow enough time for people to meet each other and talk. And yet, when we tried to do some kind of activities in the beginning so that they'd know each other better, they would not. Like introduce your neighbor—that kind of thing—no, they'd have nothing to do with it. The only thing I can identify at this point is a very, very strong religious thing going with them. They have so many church meetings and sometimes that's what they want to talk about when I get in the homes.

There is one person in the group who has been calling people and hassling them about rates being too low. She has a distinctive voice and if she saw an ad in the paper and if it was fifteen dollars a week, she'd call them and chew them out for giving care for that amount, and that's coming back to me now. They have been very suspicious of getting into a group with this particular person.

A training educator makes some comparisons:

The people out there in the very tight suburban middle-class area want to be *told*. They're so much into this thing of being told how to do things, and I see some of that in the group I'm working with now.

It's really hard to get them to say, "I don't like that." And when they say, "that makes me angry" or "I think that group last night was really dumb"—when you get to that point and they don't feel there has to be a resource person to come in telling them how to do it, you've really got some progress. But it's really difficult in those suburban areas.

I think it's true because they were brought up in our school system and were told how to do things, and they did it. They had a report to do, and they did it. They had a project to do, and they did it by that time. And if you want to know something else, you go to someone who's got letters after his name. One of the groups in our project, the field worker was halfway chided by the group for not going out and getting people who have Ph.D.s or M.A.s to come out to be the resource leader. They did not want to be their own resource leader—at least not at the beginning. I think even at the end it was true of that group and it was because of the suburban, middle-class kind of thing. It's just hard to get through that.

When they were given a chance to set some of their own evenings, they just sat there, not knowing what to do. It's like a muscle that's not used. If you don't exercise your choice muscles they atrophy. I think most of them in that situation work through conflict with the parents just as well as anyone else, but when they go into a group or a class situation, then they want to be told how to do it. Sometimes in a home-visitor role when you go in to demonstrate how to use toys or read aloud, the day care mother takes off to make the beds or something, or goes to the store. You have to set it up in the very beginning. You have to make it clear, "I'm not here to do activities with just the children. We'll work them through together." I think when you both work with the children, you can talk through some things they're doing and can be a model while working with the children.

Not all the field workers, only one, had the experience of being a day care mother. I think it's an advantage to have had this experience because there's such a difference between the hassles that you have in a home and the hassles that you have in a center. You have your own family to deal with when you've got problems with the day care kids—or maybe your husband hates the fact that you're doing day care—so I think it makes it easier to listen to some of those problems. Working with the parents and with the day care children is often one of their requests for cluster night. They used to ask for some kind of child growth and development, discipline, first-aid. More and more we're seeing groups asking, "How do you talk with parents and deal with parents?"

A staff member of a child care agency says:

We feel training is important but we feel we're not at the point where that's a major thing. We've also talked about having some resources on communication skills or sensitivity training, or getting the expertise we have from someone here who does a lot of outreaching and would do a workshop for that. Or, the guilt thing of leaving your kids, to help caregivers realize that the other mothers, the users, may have these feelings even if they don't, and can't figure out why there's trouble. We did a workshop on the unattached child and got into that a little bit from the child's point of view of being shuffled around and forming no attachment.

An educator, employed in a health service and affiliated with a Day Care Association, said:

We had a week long preservice workshop that we conducted here and used our nursery school. We had our psychologist, nutritionist, nurse—you know, all the standard kind of things. We made it nine to four or nine to three. Almost all had had experience. We approached it that the caregivers were people who were already experts in caring for children. We made sure that each expert psychologist that came in would deal with the group that way so it was a real legitimate kind of workshop. We picked up a lot of things in the group situation—I sat in, the social worker sat in—that we could earmark that maybe this person needed help in some of these areas that we didn't pick up in the individual interviews.

We also have evening workshops. We had job duties for day care mothers and they are expected to attend monthly meeting workshops. We split them into two groups and had psychologists and all that in a session. I teach the whole thing—it makes them feel part of the agency, gives a day care mother a chance to share with other day care mothers so that she doesn't feel she's out there alone, etcetera. Then we had the individual visits by social workers.

We got the idea of this course going partly because I'm an academic person, and partly to have something that was sort of toward sub-certification. The problem was, what benefit would it be to day care mothers—they wouldn't be getting more money. We thought of trying to change the law so they could take more children, but some of the day care mothers wiped that out—"Who wants to take more kids. We want to get more money for the same number of kids." We talked to some people who'd done a training program in another part of the state and to some people at the community college. We used as a principle of the course the things they couldn't get in the community and that were not easy to get, and that were specifically for home day care people.

We had some community meetings and some of the women who came had been in another training program which had been available some time ago. Many of them said they enjoyed the files they'd been given then and the getting together with other day care mothers, some of whom weren't licensed at that time but who became licensed. They'd bring out the information file, clearly reminiscent of those meetings—how great they were and how they really enjoyed sharing what went on, the context of how the meetings were set up including kids sometimes and husbands sometimes, natural parents sometimes—a lot of dynamics. One woman was saying that the thing she enjoyed most was having the natural parents come in and say what they didn't like about her and it was an open discussion. People tend to close the door when it comes to things like that, depending on the person, but I've come to the conclusion it's true of more people than not: with the protection of the group they'll speak their minds more than when they're just talking with each other daily.

I think the training program they talked about should have screened the participants more in that most of them should have been people new to day care or who wanted to start day care. Most of them turned out to be people that had been in day care for a while, and some of them had even had earlier training. What we're developing our course for is for people who want to get into day care but want to know a little bit more before they do it. And if after they go through it, they don't want to get into it, that's okay.

Another thing about federally funded training programs is that they won't be here forever and that's the other reason I saw to have our course at the community college—which can there on a constant basis to be a constant support and it says to the community that these people are there—and use that as a combination support system with some of the people from health and education and social services. All we need to do is get more publicity and we're on our way to having a good system.

Many women are doing day care because their husbands do not want them to work in an office or a school, whatever, until the kids are in school. A lot of them have trouble getting out at night to these courses. Some of these ladies have had open confrontation with their husbands—it's kind of a women's lib process. You don't really want to start trouble, but some of these ladies have done more thinking than in a long time.

What I see happening is that people initially started through some kind of earlier training program say, "That's not good enough. I want to go down and take some child development classes." Because people in their thirties are not going to mess around with this kind of program—they want some actual kind of training. We feel pushed here by the day care mothers themselves, to say that the state has to say, "You need some child development classes when you start taking care of children, and you need a first-aid class." There's a push from all over the state by day care mothers to have the standards raised for licensing.

This has been more of an awareness or consciousness-raising program than education in the sense that "Now you're done with our one-hundred-dollar course, now you're this kind of a person." I think we've really tried to get away from that, from saying, "You're not adequate—you take our one-hundred-dollar program and then you will be adequate"; but rather to use this as a forum to allow the network to become self-conscious so the day care mothers in a particular area know who the other ones are and so they can call them. They've met them, worked with them in groups, and feel comfortable in calling them saying, "I'm ill. Can you take one of my day care kids?"

It was a lot of help that the deputy director of the community college agreed to the course for no tuition, which was rough on his budget, but he thought it was such a good idea—see, he's in this community service program so he can support new things—and we impressed him with the fact that day care mothers don't have much money and they may not come out if they have to pay a lot. So he said it would be for free, and for credit and could begin in January.

So we went ahead and got the list of things the day care mothers had wanted, and used the principles I mentioned to form the course. Then we rested, and we rested a week too long or something. They got some politics going there. He apparently had not checked it out with the people in early-childhood even though the gal from that department had been at the meeting. They were all a little irresponsible in following through in checking-out process. We called up to set a meeting and they said they'd listed another course. Jane, from early-childhood, was going to write the curriculum and would teach it all, and it was not going to be free because it would be in the early-childhood division.

We were furious. Jane said, "There's nothing that can be done but I'll be willing to meet with you." She had her whole thing right there, her curriculum, her supervisor, and the guy who'd made the agreement with us. The sparks were flying—it was the most political meeting. I made it straight; I said, "I don't want politics to get in the way of day care and these are politics. Look at this course outline." And he took Jane's and put it at the bottom of the pile and said, "What's your curriculum?" And they accepted it. Then they had the problem of money and the credits. The supervisor said, "We can give it free and noncredit," and I said, "Listen, one of the things on the curriculum you accepted is building up the self-image of the day care mother and I think it's ridiculous not to offer credit when this is one of the things you're trying to do.". . .

They accepted our curriculum because it was an introductory course and doesn't have to be that formal. We accepted that, after this point, day care mothers may want to take more child development and other things that fit right into their offerings. But this has got to be good, and can't just be thrown together. We're only going to have one grab at some of these people and they better do it right. It can't be a turn-off with one person lecturing. We're going to get the people like the social worker from Tri-County who used to be director of a day care center; screening technicians who work in the health department, who are very down-to-earth people with skills at training people in health; and for the ones that are more day-care-oriented, we'll have day care mothers. We see educational TV as the next step. What I see our course doing, if this becomes established, is challenging other community colleges to do a similar thing.

The Director of a training project that grew out of a small, largely volunteer, information and referral service and was carried on under a federal grant reports on her first year's experience:

We learned a lot from the training sessions we ran. Like the one in the black community—even though I grew up on the fringes of it, I never really understood it. The most help to me was my twins—I could have had five Ph.D.s and it wouldn't have mattered, but when we introduced each other around the room and I said, "I'm the mother of twins," that did it!

We're getting better at the recruitment for our training courses—in fact we're getting so good we get masses of people. In Chinatown where we ran them with interpreters, we had almost forty people and another thirty more on the waiting list for the second Chinese session. We didn't come "white-faced us, we'll show you"—we let the community do it. We spent January and February, every day, in Chinatown making contacts with every single self-help, every community radical or straight organization you can imagine and educated them as to what family day care was. Did they have it in Chinatown? Did they want it? What did they think of it? Would they like to work with us? We got a group of people really fired up. The experts who are actually doing the workshop—we trained them. We had Chinese lunches telling them, "You don't lecture, you listen, you encourage discussion." We wrote up the atmosphere. We basically held their hands saying, "You can do it."

I've been feeling like a giant dummy the last four months because I don't speak Chinese. I learned some in the course of this but not a whole lot. I went to the first session and here are all these people and I'm sort of saying my thing in English and Donna's translating. That was the first week. we got a very sharp social worker who had been the director of a day care center in Chinatown. She's now in a very clinical, postdoctoral Ph.D. program—I suspect a little bit lonely for the community so this has been great for her. We were really lucky to have gotten her.

We pay the day care mothers three-seventy-five per session for coming, clearly an incentive. Especially in Chinatown, they desperately need money. They're taking care of kids anyway, many of them. We haven't promised them jobs, we make it very clear that this is something they can do, but we aren't going to pay—"It's an arrangement between you and the child's parents. We can't at the office, not speaking Chinese, promise that we'll find you children." But what's happening is that all these agencies, whether it's Chinese Newcomers, the Drop-In Center, the other child care center—they all have enormous waiting lists, multitudinal requests for family day care or babysitting which they haven't been able to really deal with. So now what we can say to the people is, okay, the Chinatown Community Children's Center will give your name to people on their waiting list, so that in essence we're kind of setting up a whole—their own—information and referral service. The fact that they're getting to know each other, that they're coming together to share their ideas and concerns is what's important to me. Sometimes we feel our major role in life is mimeographing things in Chinese.

In the last five years there are many people from Hong Kong. We didn't plan to do this Chinese thing—what we were going to do is a kind of bilingual, all-together one, never dreaming we would have this much response from the Chinese community. The group we've been doing the last few weeks has been the hardest because those women don't really speak any English. They chatter in Chinese the whole time, or they bring their uncle who translates for them. And we have all these tape recorders going, translating from Mandarin to Cantonese—it gets to the point we're shouting, "Now the insurance...." We also had all these babies, we have free child care downstairs. The last week it wasn't really a hassle having them, they've adjusted.

A licensing staff director tells about another culture:

The Mexican-American day care mothers love kids, they really do love them. Motherhood means a lot to the real Mexican family—a lot of these women haven't joined the liberation movement bit....

Sometimes the Mexican-American day care mothers call. The way I like to recruit is through certified mothers. They know of someone and that way we have a pretty good idea of what they're like. I have three that are in a family, that are related—either mothers and daughters, sisters or in-laws.

In our building we have no room to have group meetings, so we have to scrounge around in the community, but it's a good thing when you have to be pushed to do this. There are worlds that are ready for you. We find Saturday, nine to ten A.M., is the best time for our workshops to begin. We can have a place free in the park with plenty of parking. The university extension is a good resource. The milk fund gave us pencils. We're pretty good beggars. We get all kinds of things. . . .

There's a certain shyness among the day care mothers. They're really reluctant to tell about the lovely things they do. Everytime they tell us it's a surprise. We had a panel one year and asked different mothers that had worked with children with certain handicaps like the retarded, physical handicaps, behavioral problems, some problems they'd had with the mothers, to show how they'd worked them out. When we certified, we knew some of them had retarded children of their own or grandchildren. There was one deaf-mute child needing care and it so happened that in one family their kids had learned sign language at school. There was a lady in her fifties who had been born and raised in Mexico and she was very much on herbs and it so happened that the university hospital here has in the last two years begun to explore the medicinal advantages of herbs and they used this woman as a resource. She was glad to tell in her very broken English about some of the experiences she's had. Really, we're so rich in resources.

We have quoted at such length to show what great possibilities there are for the entire field—even for the sponsoring institutions—for promoting new ideas and continuing growth. It is impressive that in many instances family day care training has not had the stultifying effect of other efforts to give additional information to already talented practitioners. Family day care training seems to be sensitive to the real needs and wishes of its clientele, and to be willing to experiment in many ways and even in many languages! Primarily, training has the potential for raising the status of family day care for practitioners as well as the community.

ENVOI

We hope we have been able to convey our enthusiasm for the many interesting and imaginative programs that are developing today in family day care. What seemed of paramount importance to us was that there seemed to be a marked trend toward greater cooperation between the private and public family day care programs which have for so many years been isolated from each other. It seemed to us that there was a new spirit of mutual trust and cooperation which both systems were finding exciting and stimulating.

It is impossible to predict the trends of the future for day care, but we venture to say that it is firmly established as an American custom that will continue whatever the economic climate. And we believe that it will increase its already great potential for providing for the fundamental needs of families, children, and the community in direct ratio to the further cooperation of services for everyone. As the lines that used to divide family day care for the poor from other family day care fade, or are actively erased, much time and talent may be freed to continue the search for solutions to inevitable problems.

It may well be that other services will follow the lead of family day care toward greater trust between the public and the private sector, with more truly universal and democratic ways of helping each other.

INDEX

Abuse: *See* Child abuse and neglect
Accountability, problems of: 114, 124
Adjustments, of children: 11, 20–21, 35, 130
Age: in playgroups, 27; routine, for school-age children, 21
Aid to Dependent Children (A.D.C.): 34, 38, 42
Area to be served: 77, 87
Arrangements: in case of sickness, 8–9, 132; discipline, 14, 15; food, 15; with friends, 17; hours, 12–13, 22; laundry, 9; money, 9, 12, 14, 21, 22, 132, 135; sharing of toys, 14; travel distance, 18; vacations, 8, 12, 14, 36
Associations: as communication, 108; development of, 58–59; focus and direction of, 61–62, 70–71; forming, 63, 122–123; and licensing, 60–61; providing models, 62–63; in public housing, 63–64; and regulations, 60; setting standards for givers, 59–60; using informal sessions, 63–64; various functions of, 59–71; WATCH, 64–70

Babysitter: defined, 16–17*n*
Black community: 134
Bulletins: 108

Career Mothers: 42
Caregivers: *See* Givers of day care
Child abuse and neglect: 104–105, 113, 114, 116
Children: adjustment to day care arrangements, 11, 130; essentials of good care for, 115–116; in foster home programs, 40; of giver's family, 20–21, 35; handicapped, 136; of permissive parents, 18; responsible, 18; safety and, 18, 113; sharing toys, 14
Child Welfare, Office of: 42
Chinese community: 134–135
"Cluster home" concept: 42
Collins, Alice H.: 72*n*
Communal child care: 29–33; advantages, 30
Communication: building a bridge for users and givers, 46–49; bulletins and newsletters, 108; license bureaus, 47; making services known, 88–89; reaching community, 109; using Associations, 108
Community: benefits for, 52, 136; reaching the, 109, 132
Community colleges: 132–133
Community Family Day Care Project: 64–67
Confidentiality of records: 89–90
Consultants: *See* Social-work consultant

Co-op child care exchanges: advantages of, 30; formalizing, 23–24; member viewpoint, 24–25; organizing, 23–25; rotating, 26–27

Counseling: by Day Care Neighbors, 94–96; in referral services, 54

Day Care Council: 49

The Day Care Exchange Project: 1*n*, 3, 75*n*

Day Care Neighborhood Service: area and population to be served, 77–78; assessing need for, 77; cost of, 80–82; description of, 72–76; finding Day Care Neighbors, 82–88; future of, 108–112; importance of record-keeping, 80; inception of, 76; informal development of, 74, 110; making it known, 88–89; operating, 88–109; planning, 76–88; realistic expectations in, 78; size of, 78; space requirements, 82; staff, 79–80, 81; termination of care, 106–107; timing the organization of, 93; using familiar arrangements, 93–94; using for referral, 95–96, 111–112, 123. *See also* Day Care Neighbors

Day Care Neighborhood Service: A Handbook for the Organization and Operation of a New Approach to Family Day Care (Collins and Watson): 72*n*, 109–110

Day Care Neighbors: 4, 56, 73; characteristic attitudes of, 98–99; and child abuse, 104–105; concept of, 110, counseling by, 94–96; dealing with unsuitable users and givers, 105–106; dependence on consultants, 96–97; discontinuing use of, 107; finding, 82–85, 123; initial contact with, 83–85; initial phases of work, 74–75; interviewing, 87–88, 90–91, 92; keeping track of neighborhood activity, 89–92; as link in referrals, 95–96, 123; maintenance difficulties, 100–103; mapping the neighborhood, 91–92; meeting licensing requirements, 74; men as, 73*n;* payment to, 81; recruiting, 79–80, 82–88; relationship with social-work consultant, 88, 92–93, 96–100, 111; role of, 88–89, 104–105; skills needed, 85, 89–90; status of, 95; taking an official role, 93–94; and termination of care, 106–107. *See also* Day Care Neighborhood Service

Day nurseries: 2, 38–39, 42–43; licensing regulations for, 113, 114

Discipline: counseling on, 95; in family day care, 14, 15; WATCH position papers on, 67–68

Divorced parents: *See* Single parents

Elderly persons, as givers: 106
Employment offices: 48, 93
Ethnic groups: 134–136
Exchanges: *See* Co-op child care exchanges
Extended family: 16–17, 19, 49

Family day care: advocates, 46; Associations and, 71; benefits of, 1; by choice, 1; description of, 1–4; development of, 16; finding, 13, 15–21; frictions in, 20, 21; funding and, 2, 33, 125; illustrations of, 4–15; informal, 1–22; licensing and, 47, 114, 124; by necessity, 1; need for, 1, 2; and numbers of children, 19,

131; with professional services *(see* Day Care Neighborhood Service); raising status of, 136; statistics, 2; transitory character of, 117. *See also* Day Care Neighborhood Service; Public family day care; Training programs
Field Study of the Neighborhood Family Day Care System: 1n, 18
Food: 15
Foster home programs: 39, 114; measuring, 115
Foster parents: 39–40
Frictions: between two mothers, 20, 131; and time of day, 21
Friendship, in day care arrangements: 5–6, 7, 9, 10–11, 13, 22
Funding: and accountability, 114; of day care studies, 3; of day nursery programs, 2, 124; of informal family day care, 33; to license bureaus, 114, 116, 124–125; to licensed facilities, 47; of public family day care, 37–38, 41, 44–45, 46; for referral services, 51; to training programs, 124–128, 132

Givers of day care: 11–15; Associations and, 58–71; children of, 20–21, 35; elderly persons as, 106; finding, 15–21 *(see also* Referral services); and licensing, 48, 59, 117–118, 122; motivations, 5, 7, 17, 34, 132; payment, 135; personality of, 115, 125; preference in parents, 7–8, 19; professional respect for, 130–131; in public programs, 42–43; recognizing needs of, 19–21; regulations and, 60, 115; suitable, 124; unsuitable, 105–106; welfare mother as, 34–37. *See also* Day Care Neighbors

Guilt feelings: 130

Handicapped children: 136
Health conditions: 113, 114, 116
Housework: 37

Illness: 8–9, 132
Information: accuracy of, 54; developing comprehensive service, 52–55; and increased licensing efforts, 118; informal methods of, 49–52; keeping current, 55; pamphlets on, 52; satellite, 55–57; using day care centers for, 48–49, 111–112. *See also* Referral services
Information—Giving and Referral: 52
Inspection: 47, 114, 115, 117; and noncompliance, 119–120
Interviews: between consultants and Day Care Neighbors, 84–88, 92; in public family day care, 40–41; record-keeping of, 89–90; spacing, 96; taping, 90–91

Laundry: 9
License bureaus: as communication, 47–48; funding to, 47, 116, 118, 124; organizing, 116; staff, 47; using for information and referral, 118, 122
License regulations: drafting, 114; efforts to revise, 120–121; formal complaint mechanisms, 122; intention of, 116; and noncompliance, 119–120; public education to: 121–122; setting standards for, 113, 116, 132
Licensing: 47, 54, 124; accountability and, 114; Associations and, 60–61; attitude of givers toward, 117, 132; cost of, 118; Day Care Neighbors and, 74; delays, 120; growth of, 40,

113–115, 118; and the law, 114, 119–120, 124; paperwork, 120; percentages, 118; positive results of, 118–123; problems and pitfalls of, 115–118; purpose of, 113; registration instead of, 122; and regulations of the past, 114; and training programs, 125; usefullness for givers, 48, 59, 122; *vs.* unlicensed care, 114, 118

Licensors: organizing Associations, 122–123; responsibility of judgment, 115–116; and staff limitations, 117, 119–120, 124; views on inspection, 115, 117, 119

Maintenance problems, between givers and users: 100–103
Men: as day care fathers, 127; as Day Care Neighbors, 73*n*, 86
Mexican-American community: 135–136
Model Cities program: 49
Money arrangements: 9, 12, 14, 135; prompt payment, 21. *See also* Funding
Mothers: *See* Givers of day care; Parents; Working mothers

Napping: 35
Newsletters: 51, 108

Operating permits: 47

Pamphlets: on day care, 1*n*, 18, 26–28, 72*n*, 109–110; on referral services, 52
Parents: guilt feelings of, 130; meeting standards of, 48; and opportunity for open discussion, 131; preferences of, 7, 18; recognizing judgment of, 119. *See also* Working parents; Single parents; Working mothers

Part-time consultants: 81
Payment: *See* Funding; Money arrangements
Permissiveness: 18
Playgroups: advantages of, 30; age range, 27; cost, 28; organizing, 25–29; publications on, 26–28; size of, 26; staff, 28; suitable space for, 28
Playgroups—Do It Ourselves Childcare: 26–27
Playgroups: How to Grow Your Own: 27–28
Politics: 133
Poor: 37, 38, 46, 118
Provider Mothers: 42
Public family day care: Community Family Day Care Project, 64–67; evolution of, 37–40; funding of, 37–38, 44–45, 46; future of, 40–45; licensing and, 120; models in, 44; need for, 46; payment, 41; process of, 41–41; as a training program of women, 42; welfare mother as giver, 34–37
Public housing projects: day care in, 43–44; promoting Associations in, 63

Record keeping: confidentiality and, 89–90; in Day Care Neighborhood Service, 80, 85, 86–87, 89; in exchanges, 23, 25; importance, in referral services, 53, 55, 57; during recruitment, 86–87
Recruitment: 86–87
Registration: 122. *See also* Licensing
Regulations: and attitude toward givers, 60; importance of, 54; licensing *(see* Licensing);

number of children, 19, 131; of past, 114
Referral services: using agencies to establish, 53; building communication for users and givers, 46–47; community and, 52; and counseling, 54; using Day Care Neighbors for, 95–96, 111–112; demand for, 52; developing comprehensive service, 52–55; in ethnic neighborhoods, 135; expansion of, 51, 53, 55; function of, 54; funding of, 51, 52; importance of location, 53; informal, 49–52; knowing restrictions and regulations, 54; through license bureaus, 118, 122; pamphlets on, 52; public, 52; satellite, 55–57; for single parents, 51; skills needed, 53, 57; staff, 53, 56–57
Research: methods of, 3
Restrictions: *See* Regulations
Rotating exchanges: 26–27
Rural areas: 39

Safety standards: 18, 28; and licensing, 113, 114, 115
Sales, June Solnit, 64–70
School-age children: 21
Sharing: 14
Sickness: 8–9, 132
Single parents: 2; and communal living, 32: referral services for, 51
Social class: and day care use, 37, 38, 46, 118; and trainability, 128–129
Social Security offices: 48
Social services, division of: 41, 42
Social-work consultant: 73, 79, 80; attitudes of, 99–100; dealing with unsuitable users and givers, 105–106; dependence of Day Care Neighbor on, 96–97; developing relationship with the Day Care Neighbor, 88, 92–98, 100, 111; finding Day Care Neighbors, 82–85; interviewing, 87–88, 90–91, 92; keeping the needs of special groups in mind, 94; learning about neighborhood, 91–92; part-time, 81; recruiting, 85–87; role of, 98–99, 100, 103
Social workers: 56
Space considerations: for Day Care Neighborhood Service, 82; for playgroups, 28; for referral services, 51, 53
Staff: clerical, 80, 81; Day Care Neighborhood Service, 79–80; of foster home programs, 39; in licensing departments, 47, 117; payment of, 53; for playgroups, 28; in referral services, 53, 56; skills needed, 53, 57; training of, 57; volunteers, 53, 56–57
Studies on day care: 1*n*, 3, 75*n*, 125–126

Termination of care: 21, 106–107
Toilet training: 5, 14
Training programs: agency, 58; curriculum, 125, 133–134; and expertness of givers, 130–131; in family day care, 125–136; federal funding for, 124–125, 132; federally funded studies of 126–128; in group care, 125; licensing and, 124–125; for licensing caseworkers, 61; politics in, 133; problems in, 128; in public family day care, 42; for referral staff, 57
Traveling distance: 18

United Fund: 49
Users of day care: and Associations, 71; finding givers *(see* Referral services); illustrations,

4–6, 9–11; interaction with giver, 36; reliability of, 19; unsuitable, 105–106

Vacations: 8, 12, 14, 36
Volunteers: 53, 56
WATCH (Women Attentive to Children's Happiness): 64–70; accomplishments of, 67–69; on discipline, 67–68; meetings, 69; problems, 69–70

Watson, Eunice L.: 72*n*
Welfare laws: 38
Welfare mothers: as day care givers, 34–37, 127
Women Attentive to Children's Happiness (WATCH): 64–70
Working mothers: finding day care, 17; needs of, 3, 9–11; views on family day care, 4–6; and work force, 2
Working parents: 1–22